Office 97
Made Simple

P.K.McBride

MADE SIMPLE
BOOKS

Made Simple
An imprint of Butterworth-Heinemann
Linacre House, Jordan Hill, Oxford OX2 8DP
225 Wildwood Avenue, Woburn, MA 01801-2041
A division of Reed Educational and Professional Publishing Ltd

⌖ A member of the Reed Elsevier plc group

OXFORD   BOSTON   JOHANNESBURG
MELBOURNE   NEW DELHI   SINGAPORE

First published 1997
© P K McBride 1997

TRADEMARKS/REGISTERED TRADEMARKS
Computer hardware and software brand names mentioned in this book are protected
by their respective trademarks and are acknowledged.

British Library Cataloguing in Publication Data
A catalogue record for this book is available from the British Library

ISBN 0 7506 3798 6

 Typeset by P.K.McBride, Southampton

Archtype, Bash Casual, Cotswold and Gravity fonts from Advanced Graphics Ltd
Icons designed by Sarah Ward © 1994
Printed and bound in Great Britain by Scotprint, Musselburgh, Scotland

Contents

Preface

This book is intended to be a companion to those others in this series that focus on individual Office applications – *Access*, *Excel*, *PowerPoint* and *Word Made Simple*.

Office 97 Made Simple concentrates on:

- the Office environment;
- those features and ways of working that are common to the applications;
- transferring and sharing data between applications, through copying, OLE (Object Linking and Embedding) and Binders;
- the graphing and graphical add-ons that can be used within all applications;
- Outlook, Office 97's personal (and workgroup) organiser;
- integration with the Internet, through e-mail and World Wide Web links.

The Office 97 suite contains so much, that it is not possible to cover it all in a book this size. I hope that I have included enough, and in enough detail, to give you what you need to get started and to work effectively across the applications.

To find out more about the individual components, see:

Access 97 Made Simple by Moira Stephen

Excel 97 Made Simple by Stephen Morris

PowerPoint 97 Made Simple by Moira Stephen

Word Made 97 Simple by Keith Brindley

Take note

There are two version of Office 97 – Standard and Professional. The only difference between the two is that the Professional version includes the Access database management software.

1 Office management

The Office equipment

In the last few years Microsoft Office has established itself as the leading business application software suite. Office 97, the latest version, has been rewritten to give better integration between the components, and simple access to the Internet.

The Office 97 suite contains:

 Word – a word processor that is extremely easy to use at a basic level, yet has all the features of a desktop publisher;

 Excel – a spreadsheet that is powerful enough to handle the accounts of a multi-million pound company, yet simple enough for a child to use for a school project;

 PowerPoint presentation software, for producing slideshows and accompanying handouts and notes;

 Access – a richly featured and highly powerful database management system;

 Binder – a new concept and leap forward in integration. With the Binder you can store Word, Excel, Access and Powerpoint documents in one file, and switch easily between them;

 Outlook is a comprehensive package for organising your life. It serves as a diary, job planner, address book, message centre and more... Networked users can share access to each other's planners, so that meetings can be arranged easily.

The hardware

Minimum requirements

Processor	Pentium
RAM	16 Mb
Hard disk	120 Mb (free)
Monitor	VGA 800x640

Recommended

Processor	Pentium
RAM	32 Mb
Hard disk	160 Mb (free)
Monitor	SVGA 1024x800

Take note

The main difference between the Standard and Professional editions is that the Professional edition includes Access. Most home and small business users should find that the combination of Excel and Mail Merge is enough for their data handling needs.

Minor applications

Office 97 has a large set of minor applications that are mainly run from within a major program. These include:

- software to add clip art, graphs, equations, charts, and decorative text to Word or Powerpoint documents;

- converters to read files from other word-processors, spreadsheets and databases into Office applications, and save files in formats suitable for other systems;

- graphics filters to handle many different formats;

- DataMap to display regional data from Excel and Access on maps;

- System Info to analyse your computer system.

New and Open Documents can be moved off the main menu if you prefer

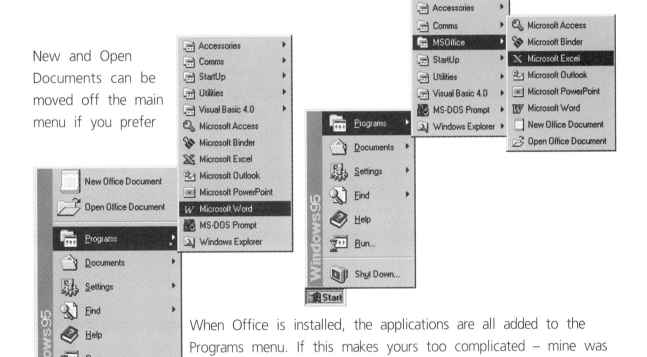

When Office is installed, the applications are all added to the Programs menu. If this makes yours too complicated – mine was very simple before! – you could to set up a new menu folder and store the Office applications there. Use **Start – Settings – Taskbar** to reorganise your Start menu.

3

Office Shortcuts

You can, of course, run all Office applications from the Start menu, but a Desktop shortcut is the quickest way into a program. With Office 97, this is taken further in the Shortcut bar, giving instant access to your applications.

● If you regularly use just one Office applications, then set up a Desktop shortcut to it.

● If you regularly use several, set up a Desktop shortcut to the Office Shortcut bar.

Basic steps

1 Run **Explorer**.

2 Switch to the **Program Files/Microsoft Office** folder.

3 Select the program.

4 Hold down the left mouse button and drag the icon onto the Desktop.

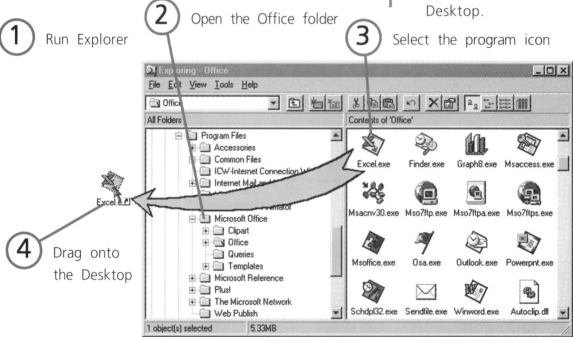

① Run Explorer

② Open the Office folder

③ Select the program icon

④ Drag onto the Desktop

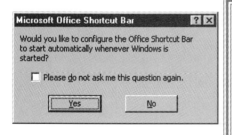

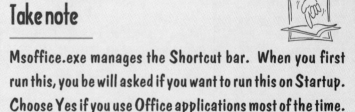

Take note

Msoffice.exe manages the Shortcut bar. When you first run this, you be will asked if you want to run this on Startup. Choose Yes if you use Office applications most of the time.

Basic steps

The Shortcut bar

□ **Moving the Toolbar**

1 Point to an empty part of the bar.

2 Drag to wherever you want it on the screen.

To place it at the top, bottom or a side, push the cursor beyond the edge of the screen.

By default, the Shortcut Bar sits at the top of the screen and contains buttons for opening or creating new files (of any Office sort), adding tasks, contacts or appointments to Outlook and for getting help. Its position and contents can be easily changed to suit your way of working.

The Bar can be a strip along any edge of the screen, or a compact block anywhere else. If it is on an edge, it can be set to Auto-hide. It will then shrink into the edge after use, and can be opened again by pointing into that edge.

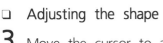

□ **Adjusting the shape**

3 Move the cursor to an edge, to get the double-arrow cursor.

4 Drag to resize.

□ **Setting Auto-Hide**

5 Click the square at the top left of the Toolbar to open the menu.

6 Click to turn **Auto Hide** on ✓ or off.

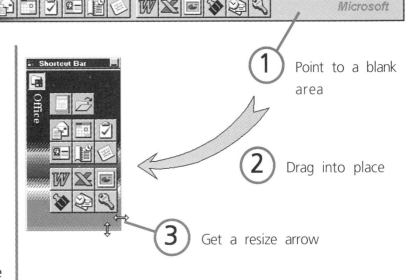

① Point to a blank area

② Drag into place

③ Get a resize arrow

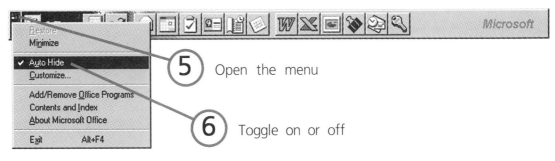

⑤ Open the menu

⑥ Toggle on or off

Customising Shortcut bars

The most useful changes you can make to the Shortcut toolbar are to add to it buttons for the applications that you use – and remove unused ones. But you can also tailor its appearance, and you should check the Settings as this tells Office where to look for Templates.

● As well as adding shortcuts from the Office set, you can also add a link to any other program on your system, or to a folder.

1 Right click on the toolbar to open the short menu.

2 Select **Customize**.

3 Open the **Buttons** panel.

4 Pick a **Toolbar**.

5 Click the □ to add ✓ or remove a button.

6 Click **OK**.

(1) Open the short menu

✓ Office
✓ QuickShelf
✓ Favorites
Programs
Accessories
Desktop
Auto Hide
Customize...
Refresh Icons

(2) Select Customize

(3) Go to Buttons

Add a button link to a program or document

(4) Select a toolbar

Add a link to a folder

Customize ? ☒ ☒

| View | Buttons | Toolbars | Settings |

Toolbar: Office ▼

Show these Files as Buttons:

------(Space)------
☑ Microsoft Word
☑ Microsoft Excel
☑ Microsoft PowerPoint
☑ Microsoft Binder
☑ Microsoft Outlook
☑ Microsoft Access
☐ Windows Explorer
☐ Internet Explorer

↑
Move
↓

Add File...
Add Folder...
Add Space
Delete
Rename...

OK   Cancel

Tip

Add buttons for the Office applications for quick and easy access to them.

(5) Tick to add as a button

(6) Click OK

Basic steps

❏ Adding Toolbars

1 Right click in a clear part of the Toolbar, to get the short menu.

2 Click on the name to add a toolbar.

❏ Creating toolbars

3 In **Explorer**, create a new folder and store in it shortcuts to your selected programs.

4 Open the **Customize** panel and select **Toolbars**.

5 Click **Add Toolbar** and browse for the new shortcut folder.

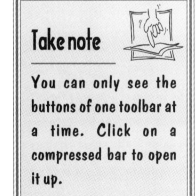

Take note

You can only see the buttons of one toolbar at a time. Click on a compressed bar to open it up.

Multiple bars

An Office toolbar represents a folder. Its shortcuts, programs and sub-folders become items on the bar.

If you like the toolbar approach, you can create your own folder of shortcuts to favourite programs and make that into a toolbar.

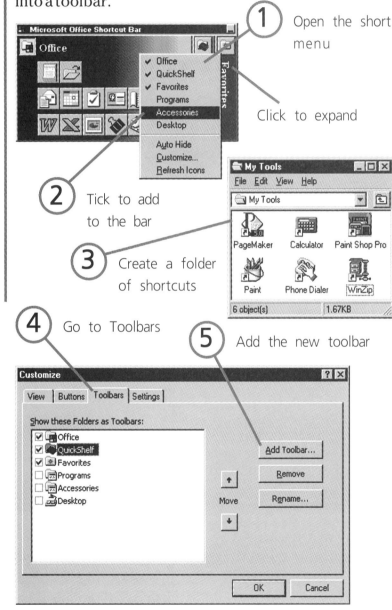

① Open the short menu

Click to expand

② Tick to add to the bar

③ Create a folder of shortcuts

④ Go to Toolbars

⑤ Add the new toolbar

Changing views

You can change the colour, button size and other aspects of the Toolbar displays, using the View panel.

The Options apply to all toolbars, though the Colour choices only apply to the selected toolbar.

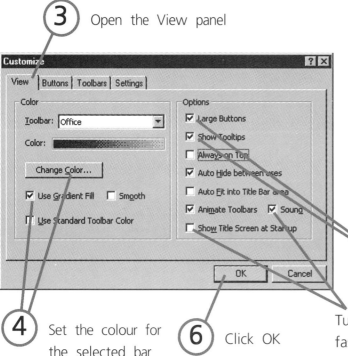

③ Open the View panel

④ Set the colour for the selected bar

⑥ Click OK

1 Right click on the Toolbar to open the short menu.

2 Select **Customize**.

3 Open the **View** panel.

4 In the **Colors** pane, select the **Toolbar** then pick the **Color** and **Fill** style.

5 Try out any **Options** that seem worthwhile – you can always reset them again.

6 Click **OK**.

These make Toolbars easier to use

Turn these off for faster working

Tip

If you want to use the Auto-Hide feature, you may find it best to locate the Toolbar on the left edge of the screen. You are less likely to activate accidentally there than at the right or bottom (close to the scroll bars) or at the top (close to the menu bar and control buttons).

Basic steps

1 Open the **Customize** dialog box if necessary.

2 Click **Settings** to open its panel.

3 Select an **Item** to change its Setting.

4 Click **Modify**.

5 Locate the folder on your system or network.

6 Click **OK** to fix the new setting.

At some point before you start to use Templates, you should check the Settings panel to make sure that Office 97 is using the right folders.

It assumes that the ready-made templates and those that you create will all be stored in the *MSOffice\Templates* folder. If you have an existing templates folder elsewhere, or want to use templates that are shared by your Workgroup, the Settings should be adjusted to match.

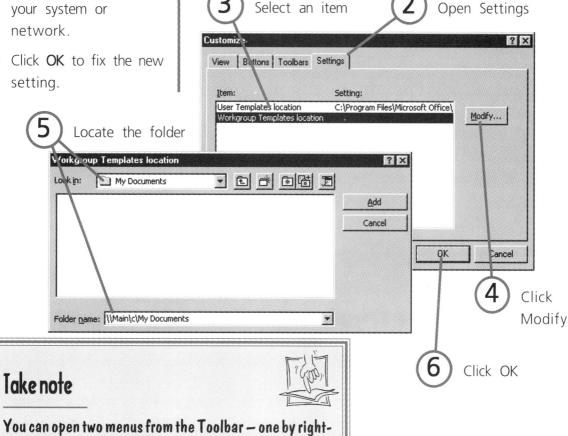

③ Select an item　　② Open Settings

⑤ Locate the folder

④ Click Modify

⑥ Click OK

Take note

You can open two menus from the Toolbar – one by right-clicking on the bar, the other by clicking the square at the top left of the bar. Customize.. and Auto Hide are in both.

Add/remove programs

After you have been using Office for a little while, you may decide that there some applications that you do not use, and which should be removed to free up space, or others which you did not install initially, but which you would now like to try.

The Setup and Uninstall routine provides a simple way to add or remove programs. It can be reached through the Shortcut bar or through the Windows 97 Control Panel.

1 Click the square at the top left of the bar to get the control menu.

2 Select **Add/Remove Office Programs**.

3 At the **Office Setup** panel, select **Office 97** and click **OK**.

4 At the **Setup** panel, click **Add/Remove**.

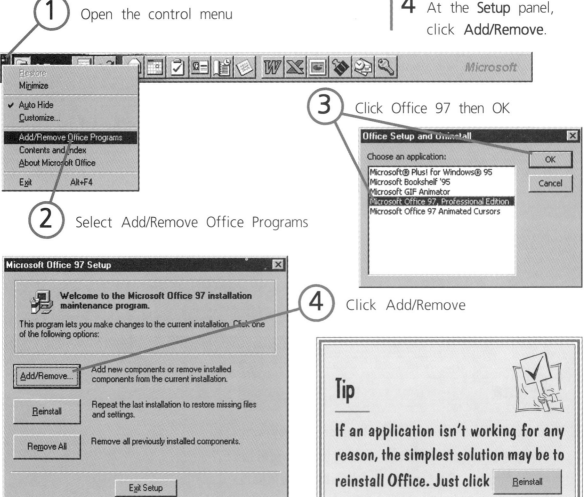

① Open the control menu

② Select Add/Remove Office Programs

③ Click Office 97 then OK

④ Click Add/Remove

Tip

If an application isn't working for any reason, the simplest solution may be to reinstall Office. Just click [Reinstall]

Selective installations

5 Select an item from the **Options** list.

6 Click **Change Options** to select elements to add or remove.

7 At the next level, if you select an item and **Change Options** is active, click it to select from its sub-set.

8 Set a tick by elements you want to include, or remove the tick from those you want to uninstall.

9 Click **OK**.

Each entry in the main Options list – and some in the second level of lists – represents a set of programs. If the box is grey, only some are installed. The Change Option button lets you select the elements you want to include.

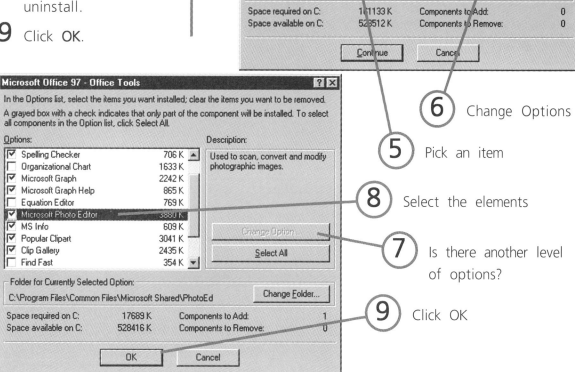

6 Change Options

5 Pick an item

8 Select the elements

7 Is there another level of options?

9 Click OK

Summary

❑ The **Office 97 suite** contains a set of major applications, plus many utilities that can be used from within the main applications.

❑ Office programs can be run from the **Start menu, Desktop shortcuts** or the **Shortcut Bar** – pick the approach that best suits your way of working.

❑ The **Shortcut Bar** can be placed anywhere on the screen, and can be set to hide itself when not in use.

❑ You can **add buttons** to the Shortcut Bar, and **link other toolbars** onto it.

❑ The **Settings panel** contains core information about the Office installation. You may need to change settings for the **Template folders**.

❑ The main programs and their many optional features can be **added or removed** at any time through the Setup and Uninstall routines.

2 Help!

Office Assistant

Seen for the first time in Office 97, Office Assistant is a friendly front-end to the Help system. It keeps an eye on what you are doing, so that, when you call on it for help, it will be ready with some likely topics. If it has guessed wrong – as it often does – you simply tell it what you need help with, and it will come up with the goods.

Tip

The Help from Office Assistant is the same as that from the Help menu.

Basic steps

1 If the Assistant is not visible, click the query icon to wake it up.

2 If a relevant topic is listed, click on it to display the page.

Otherwise

3 Type a word or phrase to describe what you want and click **Search**.

4 Click **Close**.

② Click to see a help page

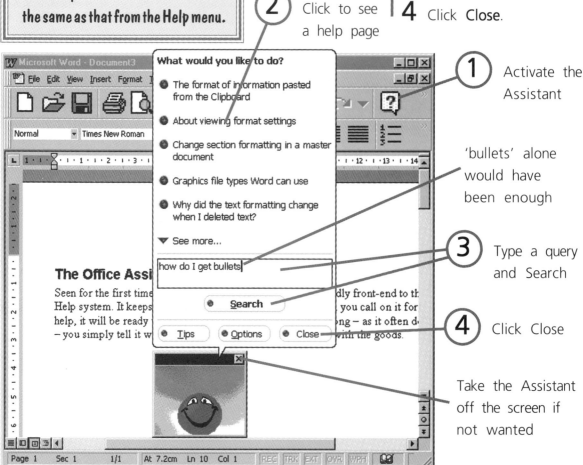

① Activate the Assistant

'bullets' alone would have been enough

③ Type a query and Search

④ Click Close

Take the Assistant off the screen if not wanted

14

Basic steps

1 Click **Options** on the Assistant's dialog or on its right-click menu.

2 Select an image on the **Gallery** panel.

3 Set the **Options** as required.

Use Next and Back to work through the set, and stop on your choice.

The Genius is the best animation.

The Logo is the least obtrusive.

Customising Office Assistant

The Assistant has nine alternative 'personalities' for you to choose from, and – perhaps more usefully – a set of options to control how it works. Have a look at them.

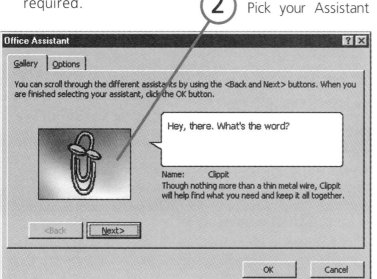

② Pick your Assistant

Office Assistant

Gallery | Options

You can scroll through the different assistants by using the <Back and Next> buttons. When you are finished selecting your assistant, click the OK button.

Hey, there. What's the word?

Name: Clippit
Though nothing more than a thin metal wire, Clippit will help find what you need and keep it all together.

<Back | Next>

OK | Cancel

③ Set options

Could be handy at first

Very useful!!

Office Assistant

Gallery | Options

Assistant capabilities
☑ Respond to F1 key   ☑ Move when in the way
☑ Help with wizards   ☑ Guess help topics
☑ Display alerts   ☐ Make sounds
☐ Search for both product and programming help when programming

Show tips about
☑ Using features more effectively   ☐ Keyboard shortcuts
☐ Using the mouse more effectively

Other tip options
☐ Only show high priority tips   Reset my tips
☐ Show the Tip of the Day at startup

OK | Cancel

The Help menu

This is the main route into the Help system. The menu has five options:

- **Microsoft Word/Access/Excel/Powerpoint Help** turns on the Office Assistant;

- **Contents and Index** opens the Help dialog, with its three panels – Contents (opposite), Index (page 18) and Find (page 20);

- **What's This?** provides quick explanations of the buttons and options on the main screen and on dialog boxes (see page 22);

- **Microsoft on the Web** offers ten links to pages at Microsoft's Web site. These are mainly for new Web users, but if you cannot find the answers you need in the built-in help – and if you have an Internet connection – you might try here;

- **WordPerfect Help** provides focused assistance for those users converting from WordPerfect. This must be installed at Setup if required.

Take note

Pressing [F1] starts up the Office Assistant.

Pressing [Shift] and [F1] activates What's This?

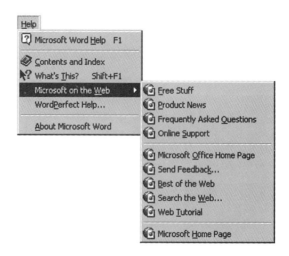

Tip

The Office applications provide help in the form of Tips. Let the pointer rest on a button for a moment and a Tool Tips will appear and tell you what the button does.

You can also have a new Tip of the Day, each time you start. See page 23 for more on this.

Basic steps

1 Click the **Contents** tab if this panel is not at the front already.

2 Click 📖 then `Display` to see the page titles.

3 Click ? then `Display` to see the page.

4 Click **Help Topics** to go back to the Contents.

or

5 Click ✕ to close the page and exit Help.

Contents

This approach treats the Help pages as a book. You scan through the headings to find a section that seems to cover what you want, and open that to see the page titles. (Some sections have sub-sections, making it a 2 or 3 -stage process to get to page titles.)

Some Help topics are stand-alone pages; others have **Related topics** buttons to take you on to further pages.

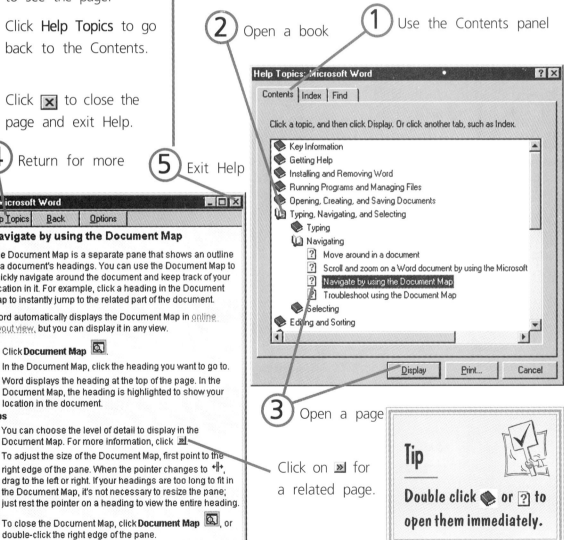

② Open a book

① Use the Contents panel

Help Topics: Microsoft Word

Contents | Index | Find

Click a topic, and then click Display. Or click another tab, such as Index.

- 📖 Key Information
- 📖 Getting Help
- 📖 Installing and Removing Word
- 📖 Running Programs and Managing Files
- 📖 Opening, Creating, and Saving Documents
- 📖 Typing, Navigating, and Selecting
  - 📖 Typing
  - 📖 Navigating
    - ? Move around in a document
    - ? Scroll and zoom on a Word document by using the Microsoft
    - ? Navigate by using the Document Map
    - ? Troubleshoot using the Document Map
  - 📖 Selecting
- 📖 Editing and Sorting

`Display` `Print...` `Cancel`

③ Open a page

④ Return for more

⑤ Exit Help

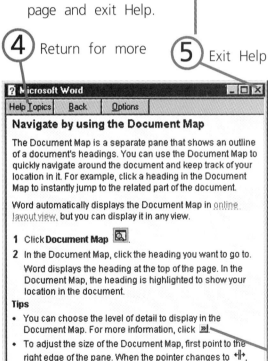

? Microsoft Word

Help Topics | Back | Options

Navigate by using the Document Map

The Document Map is a separate pane that shows an outline of a document's headings. You can use the Document Map to quickly navigate around the document and keep track of your location in it. For example, click a heading in the Document Map to instantly jump to the related part of the document.

Word automatically displays the Document Map in online layout view, but you can display it in any view.

1 Click **Document Map** 🔲.

2 In the Document Map, click the heading you want to go to.

Word displays the heading at the top of the page. In the Document Map, the heading is highlighted to show your location in the document.

Tips

- You can choose the level of detail to display in the Document Map. For more information, click ».

- To adjust the size of the Document Map, first point to the right edge of the pane. When the pointer changes to ↔, drag to the left or right. If your headings are too long to fit in the Document Map, it's not necessary to resize the pane; just rest the pointer on a heading to view the entire heading.

- To close the Document Map, click **Document Map** 🔲, or double-click the right edge of the pane.

Click on » for a related page.

Tip

Double click 📖 or ? to open them immediately.

Using the Index

Though the Contents are good for getting an overview of how things work, if you want help on a specific problem – usually the case – you are better off with the Index.

This is organised through a cross-referenced list of terms. The main list is alphabetical, with sub-entries, just like the index in a book. And, as with an index in a book, you can plough through it slowly from the top, or skip through to find the words that start with the right letters. Once you find a suitable entry, you can display the list of cross-referenced topics and pick one of those.

Basic steps

1 Click the **Index** tab.

2 Start to type a word into the slot to focus the entries list or use the scroll bar to find the topic.

3 Select the entry.

4 Click ▐ Display ▐.

5 If you offered a set of topics, click ▣ to the most suitable.

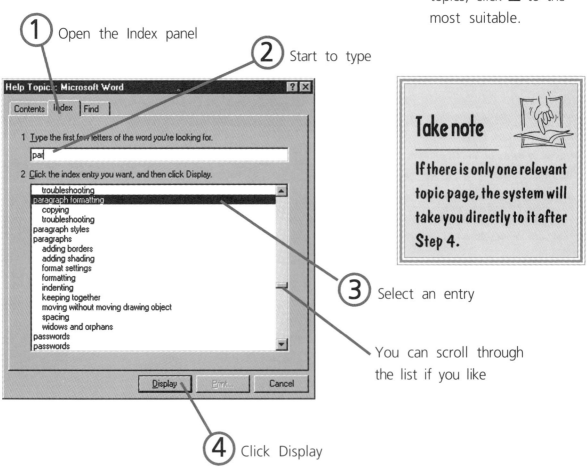

① Open the Index panel

② Start to type

③ Select an entry

You can scroll through the list if you like

④ Click Display

Take note

If there is only one relevant topic page, the system will take you directly to it after Step 4.

6 The Help page will open. When you have done you can click **Help Topics** to return to the Index, or **Back** to read the last Help page or ⊠ to exit Help.

Some Help pages use a graphical display. Click on a label to find out more about the item.

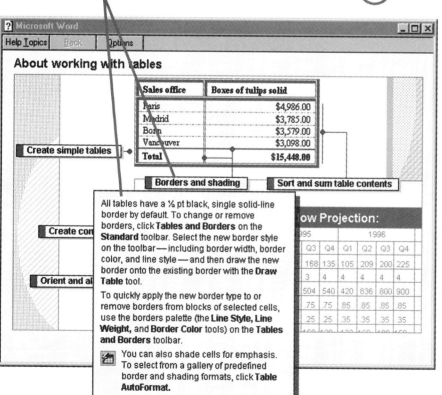

⑥ Do you want more help?

Microsoft Word

| Help Topics | Back | Options |

Troubleshoot styles

What do you need help with?

≫ A style has changed unexpectedly.

≫ Applying a style turns off bold, italic, or underlining.

≫ When I used the Style Gallery command, it didn't keep the template with my document.

≫ Paragraphs with the same style applied look different.

⑤ Pick a topic

Microsoft Word

| Help Topics | Back | Options |

About working with tables

Sales office	Boxes of tulips solid
Paris	$4,986.00
Madrid	$3,785.00
Bonn	$3,579.00
Vancouver	$3,098.00
Total	**$15,448.00**

Create simple tables

Borders and shading Sort and sum table contents

All tables have a ¼ pt black, single solid-line border by default. To change or remove borders, click **Tables and Borders** on the **Standard** toolbar. Select the new border style on the toolbar—including border width, border color, and line style — and then draw the new border onto the existing border with the **Draw Table** tool.

To quickly apply the new border type to or remove borders from blocks of selected cells, use the borders palette (the **Line Style, Line Weight,** and **Border Color** tools) on the **Tables and Borders** toolbar.

You can also shade cells for emphasis. To select from a gallery of predefined border and shading formats, click **Table AutoFormat.**

Create co...

Orient and al...

...ow Projection:

995		1996			
Q3	Q4	Q1	Q2	Q3	Q4
168	135	105	209	200	225
3	4	4	4	4	4
504	540	420	836	800	900
.75	.75	.85	.85	.85	.85
.25	.25	.35	.35	.35	.35

Tip

By default, Help pages stay on top of other windows. If you don't want this, click the Options button and turn off Keep Help on Top.

19

Finding Help

If you can't track down the help you need from the Index, you can **Find** it using the third Help panel. This works by creating a list of all the key words in the Help pages; you give it one or more words to search for and it produces a list of all the topics that contain matching words.

1 Open the **Find** panel in **Help Topics**.

2 Type your word into the top slot. As you type, words starting with the typed letters appear in the pane beneath.

3 If you want to narrow the search, go back to step 2, type a space after your first word and give another.

4 Select the most suitable word from the **Narrow the search** pane.

5 Select a topic from the lower pane.

6 Click [Display].

Use Clear if you want to start a new search

② Type the search word(s)

① Click Find

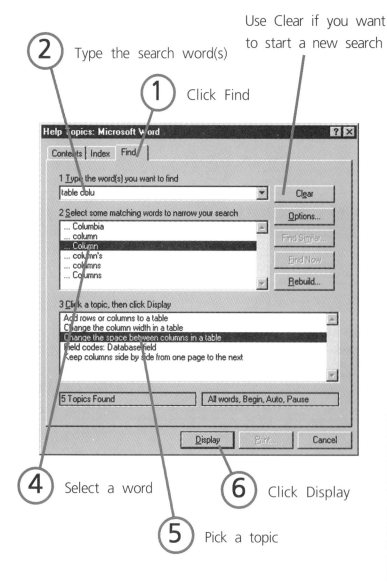

④ Select a word

⑥ Click Display

⑤ Pick a topic

Take note

Asking the Office Assistant a question produces much the same result as Using Find.

20

Basic steps

❏ **Narrowing the scope**

1 On the **Find** panel, click
  Options... .

2 On the **Find Options**
  panel, click Files... .

❏ This shows a list of the
  Help files that will be
  searched. Some of
  these are not relevant.

3 Hold **[Ctrl]** and click on
  the files that you want
  it to ignore. If you
  remove one by
  mistake, click again to
  reselect it.

4 Click **OK** then close the
  Options panel.

Take note

The first time you use
Find for any application,
a Wizard will run to create
the word list. Take the
Minimum option — it is
quicker and should do all
you want.

Find options

There are several Options that you can set to alter the
nature of the search or narrow its scope.

In the **Search for words containing** box, select:

All the words... where you are using several words to
focus on one topic;

At least one... where you are giving several alternatives in
the hope that it recognises one.

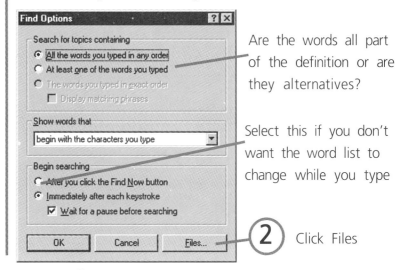

Are the words all part
of the definition or are
they alternatives?

Select this if you don't
want the word list to
change while you type

② Click Files

③ [Ctrl] and click to remove or reselect

④ Click OK

What's This?

Office's icons, menus and dialog boxes are designed to be intuitive – which is great, as long as you know how to intuit! However, when you first start to use these applications, you may need a little prompting. *What's This?* supplies those prompts for the buttons and menu items in the main application window.

Once you open a dialog box, you can no longer get to the What's This? command. However, the help is generally still at hand. Most dialog boxes have a query icon [?] at the top right of the title bar. This runs What's This?

❑ **In the main window**

1 Open the **Help** menu and select **What's This?**

❑ **On a dialog box**

2 Click on [?] or [?].

3 Click the ⬀ cursor on the item that you want to know about.

4 After you have read the help box, click anywhere to close it.

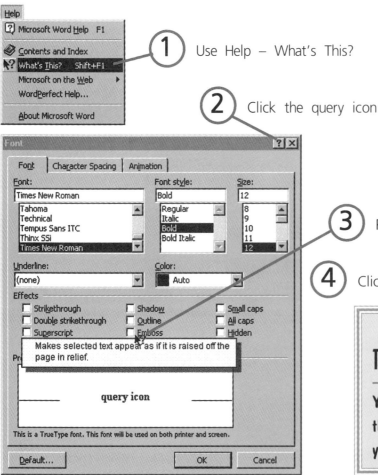

① Use Help – What's This?

② Click the query icon

③ Point and click for help

④ Click anywhere to close

query icon

Tip

Use [Shift] –[F1] for help on menu items.

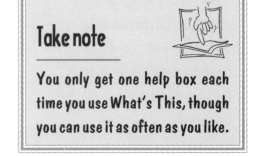

Take note

You only get one help box each time you use What's This, though you can use it as often as you like.

Basic steps

❑ **When the light goes on**

1 Click on the light icon to get the Tip.

❑ **At any time**

2 If the speech bubble is not open, click on the Assistant to open it.

3 Click on **Tips** to get the latest tip.

4 Use **Back** and **Next** to go over any past tips in the store.

5 Click **Close**.

Tip

Every time you start up, you get a **Tip of the Day**. Some tips are just for fun, others are valuable. If you want to turn them off – or have the high-priority (useful!) ones only – change the settings on the Options panel.

Tips

If ever you see 💡 on Office Assistant, it has a tip related to the last job you did – or the last error report that came up. These are stored in the Assistant, and can be scrolled back through, if necessary.

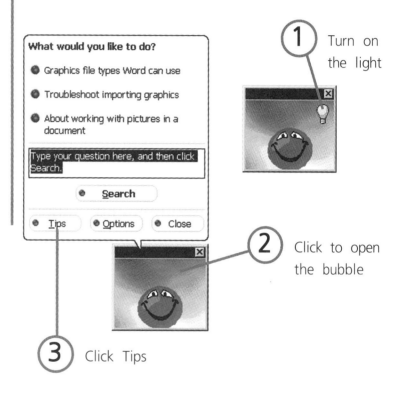

① Turn on the light

② Click to open the bubble

③ Click Tips

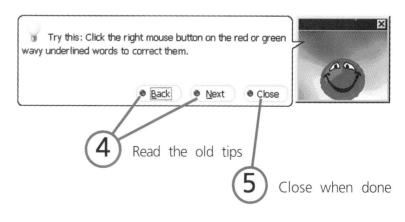

④ Read the old tips

⑤ Close when done

Summary

- ❑ Help is always available.

- ❑ **Office Assistant** is a friendly front-end to the Help system. It will offer appropriate help when needed, and can handle questions written in simple English.

- ❑ Office Assistant has several 'personalities' – choose the one that suits you.

- ❑ Use the **Contents** panel when you are browsing to see what topics are covered.

- ❑ Use the **Index** to go directly to the help on a specified operation or object.

- ❑ If you can't locate the help in the Index, use the **Find** facility to track down the pages.

- ❑ For help in a **dialog box** or **panel**, use **What's this?** or click the query icon and point to the item.

- ❑ If you hold the cursor over an **icon**, a brief prompt will pop up to tell you what it does.

- ❑ The **Tip of the Day** at start up can be switched off when no longer wanted. Tips are stored and can be reviewed at any time.

3 Common features

Menus and toolbars

The Office 97 suite is a huge and complex piece of software, yet it is straightforward to use – at a basic level. (Mastery takes time!) One of the key factors in this ease of use is that – wherever possible – the same jobs are performed using the same commands, accessed from the same buttons or menus. As there is a large core of common tasks, once you have got the hang of one application, you are on the way to mastering the next.

Menus

Commands are grouped sensibly on the menus. Browse through them to see the type of command to be found on each menu.

- An arrow to the right of an item leads to a sub-menu;
- If a menu item is followed by ... then selecting it opens up a dialog box where you specify details.

- ❑ Mouse control

1 Click on a name to drop down its menu.

2 Point to an arrowed item to open its menu.

3 Point and click to select a menu item.

- ❑ Keyboard control

4 Hold [Alt] and press the underlined letter (usually the first) to drop down the menu.

5 Use ⬇ and ⬆ to reach items, and ➡ to open sub-menus.

6 Press [Enter] or ↵ to select.

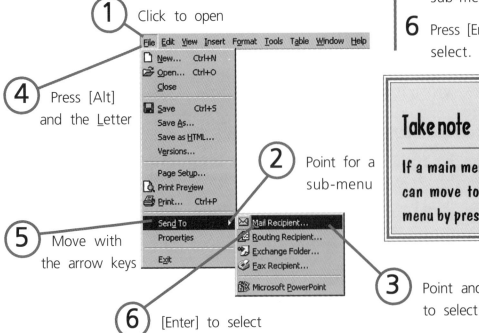

① Click to open

④ Press [Alt] and the Letter

② Point for a sub-menu

⑤ Move with the arrow keys

⑥ [Enter] to select

③ Point and click to select

Take note

If a main menu is open, you can move to another main menu by pressing ⬅ or ➡.

26

Toolbars

Take note

The toolbars' titles are taken off if you merge the bars into the window frame. (See page 29.)

The buttons on the toolbars give quick and easy access to the more commonly-used commands. Each application has half a dozen or more toolbars, many of which – with variations – are found in all.

Some toolbars are open by default, but all can be displayed or removed as required. You can also add or remove buttons from any bar. See the next page.

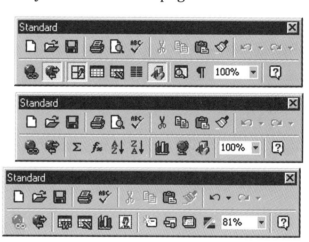

The **Standard** toolbars from Word (top), Excel (middle) and PowerPoint (bottom), hold the buttons for most commonly-used commands. Those for file handling, printing, editing, Internet access, zoom (screen magnification) and help present on all three toolbars.

Word, Excel and PowerPoint have these, though their contents vary slightly.

Formatting sets the style, alignment and layout of text.

Drawing has line and shape tools for creating diagrams.

Picture lets you control the appearance of an inserted picture.

Web turns the application into a Web browser for surfing the Internet.

Selecting toolbars

If you find toolbars useful – and you will – you can have more on screen than just the default ones. But don't overdo it. Every toolbar you add reduces the amount of visible working space!

Basic steps

❑ **Selecting toolbars**

1 Open the **View** menu.

2 Select **Toolbars**...

3 Click a name to turn its display on ☑ or off.

❑ **Customizing**

4 From the **Toolbars** menu, pick **Customize**.

5 On the **Options** panel, adjust the display to suit yourself.

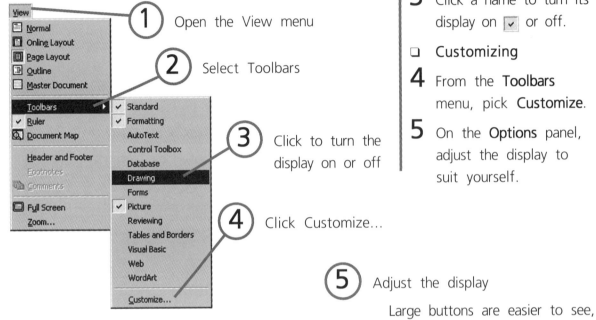

① Open the View menu

② Select Toolbars

③ Click to turn the display on or off

④ Click Customize...

A few toolbars are not on the **Toolbars** menu, but all are in the **Toolbars** panel. Add or remove any from here.

⑤ Adjust the display

Large buttons are easier to see, but take up far more space.

ScreenTips remind you what the buttons do.

Do you like to use keyboard shortcuts?

Animation is a pain in the eyes – ignore it.

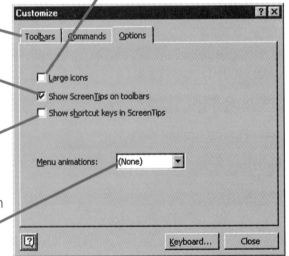

Tip

You can also open the Toolbars menu by right clicking on any toolbar.

28

Basic steps

1 Point to the title bar or to the lines at the start of the toolbar.

2 Drag the toolbar, pushing it off the edge if you want to merge it into the frame.

3 Release the mouse button.

4 Drag on an edge or corner to resize a floating toolbar.

Placing toolbars

Button toolbars can be merged into the window frame, or allowed to 'float' on the document area. The position and size of floating toolbars can be adjusted at any time.

Those bars that you want to use all of the time are probably best fitted into the frame. Those that are only wanted for the occasional job – e.g. Drawing for creating an illustration – can be brought up as needed, and floated in a convenient place.

You can drag bars within the frame, if needed

Faint arrows show that the display has been cut short

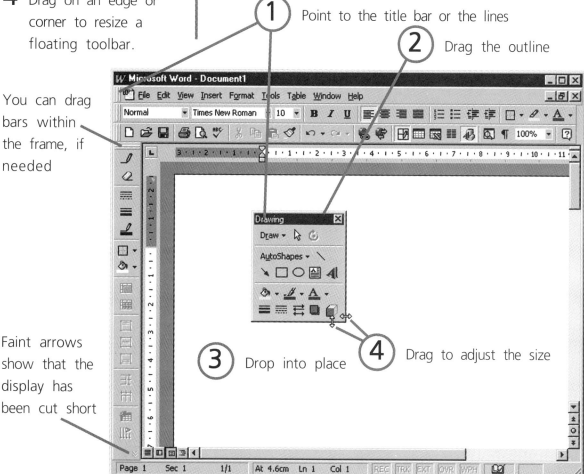

29

Adding and removing buttons

You can add buttons to, or remove them from, a toolbar that is currently on screen. New buttons can be from any category, though it helps to keep the same kind together.

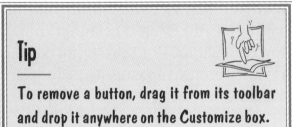

Tip

To remove a button, drag it from its toolbar and drop it anywhere on the Customize box.

Basic steps

1 On the **Toolbars** menu, select **Customize**...

2 Open the **Commands** panel.

3 Select the **Category**.

4 Select a button and drag it across the screen to the toolbar.

5 Repeat steps 3 and 4 as desired.

6 Click **Close**.

Use the I-beam to position the button

④ Drag onto a toolbar

② Open Commands

③ Pick a category

Click to find out about a chosen button

⑥ Close

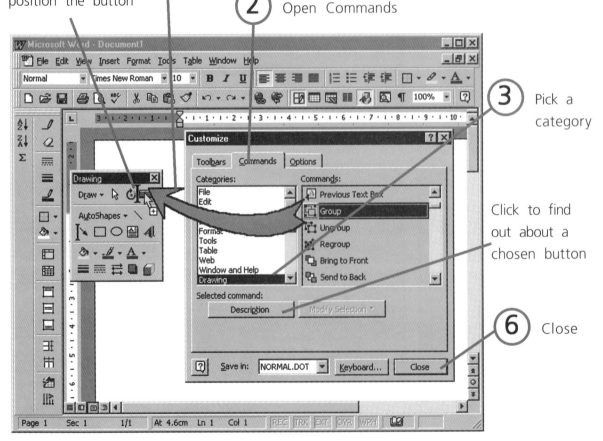

Basic steps

Custom menus

1 On the **Toolbars** menu, select **Customize**...

2 Open the **Commands** panel.

3 Click on the menu to open it for editing.

4 Select the **Category**.

5 Find the **Command** that you want to add.

6 Drag it onto the menu.

You won't want to customising menus straight away, but it is useful to know that it can be done. You might, for instance, find that you often use Charts in documents. An *Insert Chart* menu item would simplify this.

Tip

To remove an command, open the Customize box, then right click on the command, and select Delete from its shortcut menu.

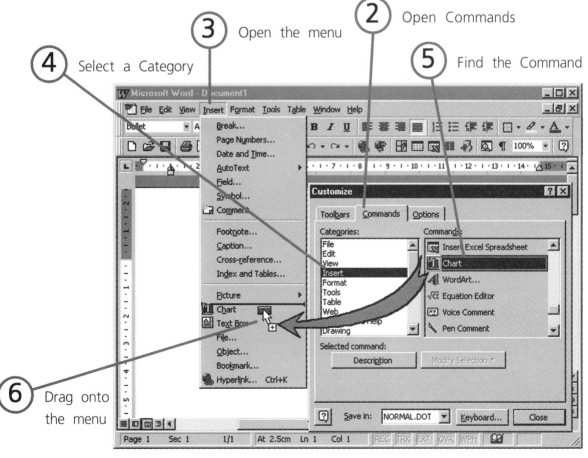

(2) Open Commands

(3) Open the menu

(4) Select a Category

(5) Find the Command

(6) Drag onto the menu

Opening files

There are several ways to open an existing Office file. Which way to take depends largely upon where you are when you start:

- If you have not yet opened the application, use 📂, the File Open shortcut, on the Office Shortcut bar or select Open Office Document from the Start menu.

- If the application is open, but you want an old file, use the File Open command or the 📂 button.

- If the application is open and the file has been used recently, open the File menu and select it from the set at the bottom of the menu.

❏ From Windows

1 Click 📂 on the **Shortcut** bar.

or

2 Click **Start** and select **Open Office Document**.

❏ From an application

3 Click 📂 on the **Toolbar** bar.

or

4 Open the **File** menu and select **Open**.

5 Select the folder.

6 Set the **Files of type** to the appropriate type.

7 If you want more details of the files, use the **Preview** or the **Properties** view.

8 Select the file and click [Open].

or

9 Open the **File** menu and select a file from the recently used list.

Click Open on the Shortcut bar

Use Start – Open Office Document

Use File – Open

Click for a recent file

32

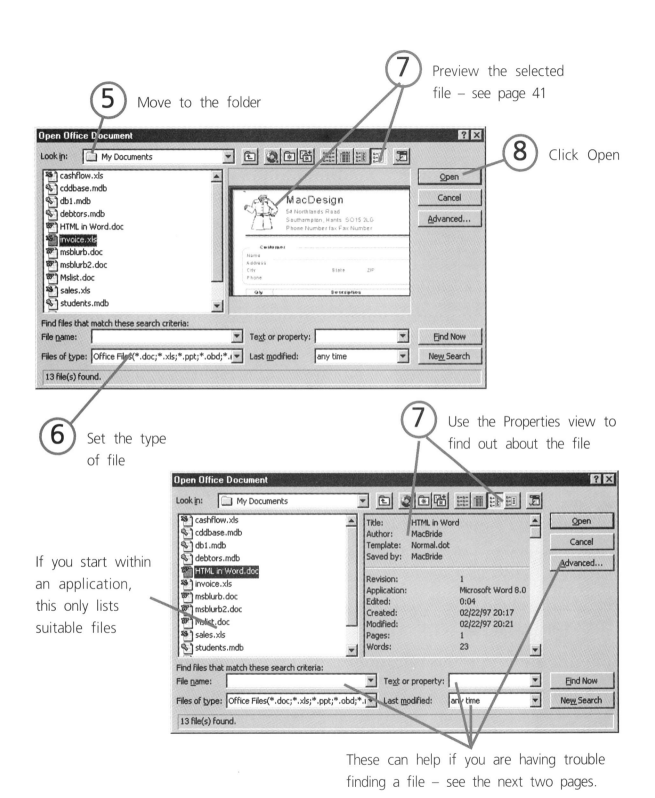

⑤ Move to the folder

⑦ Preview the selected file – see page 41

⑧ Click Open

⑥ Set the type of file

⑦ Use the Properties view to find out about the file

If you start within an application, this only lists suitable files

These can help if you are having trouble finding a file – see the next two pages.

33

Finding files

If you have a lot of files in a folder, or have forgotten a file's name, or – perhaps worse – forgotten where you stored it, Office 97 will help you to find the one you want.

At the Open dialog box, you can search on the basis of:

- **Type** – selected from the Files of type list;
- **Name** – which can use wildcards (see below);
- **Age** – when it was last saved;
- **Content** – a word or phrase in the text of the file or in its properties panel;

And if you don't know the folder, the **Advanced** options will let you run a wider search.

Finding by name

If you are sure about part of the name, type that in the File name slot. The search will find those files that contains that set of characters anywhere in the name:

e.g. '*memo*' would find '*memo* to boss.doc', '29june *memo*.txt', '*memo*ry costs.xls'

If you know the start and end of the name, but not the middle characters, fill the gap with an asterisk (*):

e.g. '*chap*2*' would find '*chap*ter2.doc', '*chap*ter20.doc', '*chap*el choir may 12.txt'

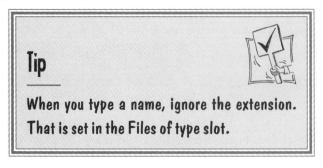

Tip

When you type a name, ignore the extension. That is set in the Files of type slot.

1 Select the folder.

2 If you know part or all of the **Name**, enter it.

3 Specify the **File type** if known, otherwise set this to **All files**.

4 If you know a word that would be found in the **Text or Properties** panel of the file, type it into the slot.

5 If you know when the file was **Last modified**, set the limit.

❑ If it isn't found...

6 Click **Advanced**.

7 Set the **Look in:** to a higher level folder, or the top of the drive.

8 Make sure that **Search Subfolders** is on.

9 Click **Find Now**.

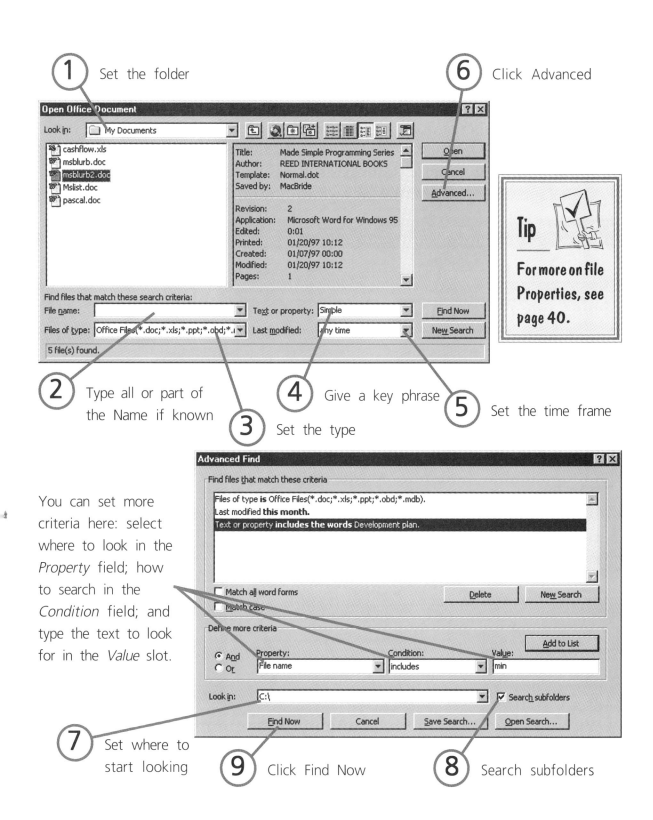

1 Set the folder

6 Click Advanced

Tip

For more on file Properties, see page 40.

2 Type all or part of the Name if known

3 Set the type

4 Give a key phrase

5 Set the time frame

You can set more criteria here: select where to look in the *Property* field; how to search in the *Condition* field; and type the text to look for in the *Value* slot.

7 Set where to start looking

9 Click Find Now

8 Search subfolders

New documents

You can start a new document from the Office Shortcut bar as well as from within applications. The document can be based on a 'blank', or on a template or wizard. These offer the same end-products – attractive, effective documents, spreadsheets and presentations, for very little effort – but approach them from different ways.

Basic steps

1 Click the **New document** button on the Shortcut bar.

or

2 Pull down the **File** menu and select **New**.

3 Open the appropriate panel.

4 Select a template or wizard.

5 Click **OK**.

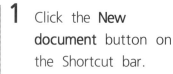

① Click New Document

② Use File – New

If you upgraded from Office 95, its templates will be here

The Previews are small but useful

③ Open the panel

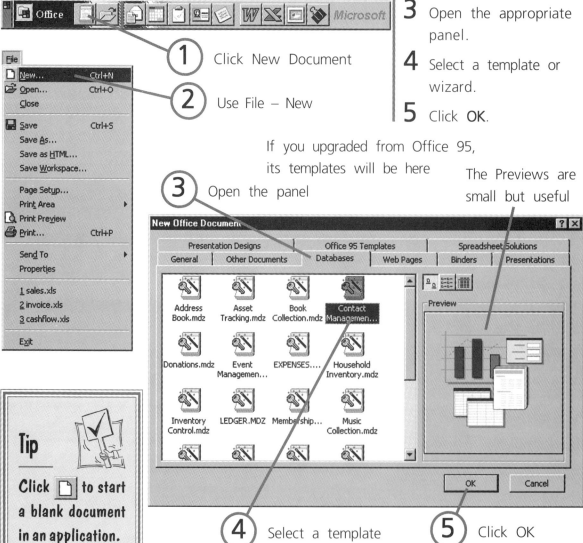

④ Select a template or wizard

⑤ Click OK

Tip

Click 🗋 to start a blank document in an application.

Templates and wizards

Fonts, styles and layouts are already in place

Templates are designed and formatted layouts with 'Click here to enter...' prompts wherever your own data is needed; Excel templates also have appropriate headings and formulae.

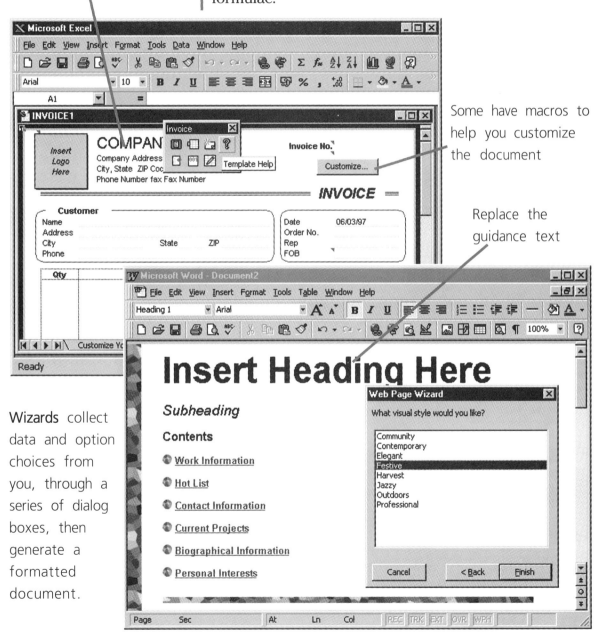

Some have macros to help you customize the document

Replace the guidance text

Wizards collect data and option choices from you, through a series of dialog boxes, then generate a formatted document.

Saving files

There are two file-saving routines in Office applications.

● **Save** is used to save an existing file after editing

● **Save As** is used to save a new file, or to save an existing file with a new name or in a new folder.

Basic steps

❑ **Save As**

1 Click 🖫 to save a new file.

or

1 Open the **File** menu and select **Save As** to save a file with a new name or location.

2 Set the **Save in** folder.

3 Enter the **Filename**.

4 Change the **Save as** type setting only if the file is to be transferred to a different system.

5 Click ▭ **Save** ▭.

6 Return to editing, or exit, as desired.

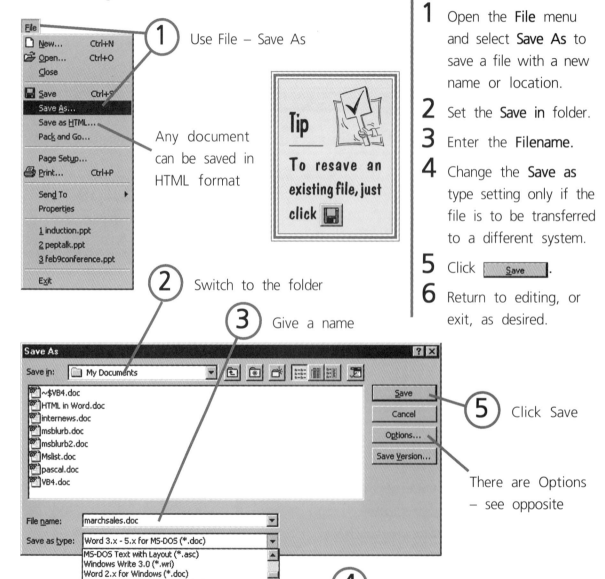

Use File – Save As

Any document can be saved in HTML format

Tip

To resave an existing file, just click 🖫

Switch to the folder

Give a name

Click Save

There are Options – see opposite

Set the type if different

Save options

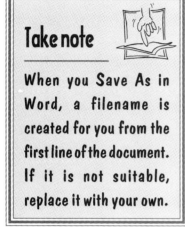
These vary between the applications. Word has an extensive Options panel; Powerpoint has a simple one; Excel's is even simpler!

Word and Excel offer three levels of protection:

Password to open, prevents all unauthorised access;

Password to modify allows anyone to read it, but only the password holder can save it, with the same name;

Read recommended sets no password, but does not allow the file to be saved, except with a new name.

If you have any doubts about the PC's reliability, turn on the **Always create Backup** option

PowerPoint also lets you **Embed True Type fonts**, to ensure that the document looks the same on any PC.

Background saves guard against lost work – but set it to a reasonable interval

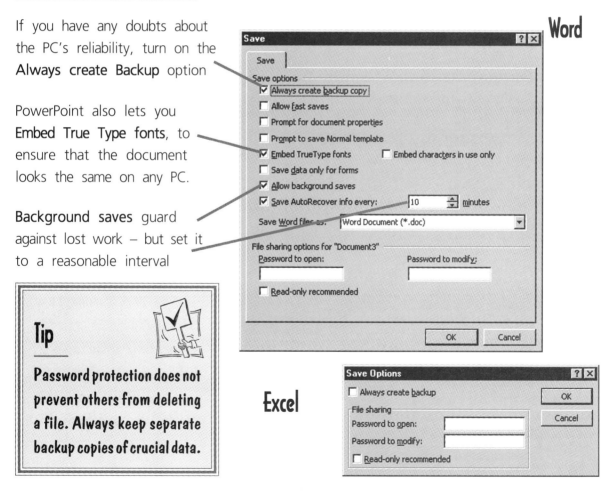

File properties

When looking at the File Find facility, we saw that you can check the nature of a file by reading its Properties panels.

- The **General** panel holds the basic details of the file – location, size, date saved, etc.;

- The **Statistics** panel (below) has a more complete set of figures – the Word Count is useful for students, journalists or anyone else working to a set limit;

- Some of the information on the **Summary** panel (opposite) is produced by Office 97; some you have to supply yourself;

- The **Contents** can be used to list the titles of slides in a presentation, or sheets in an Excel book;

- The **Custom** panel can hold details of fields within the document – this is for advanced users only!

Basic steps

1 Open the **File** menu and select **Properties**.

2 Use the **Summary** panel.

3 Enter information as required – the **Subject** and **Keywords** will be useful in future Finds.

4 Turn on **Save Preview Picture** if this will help to identify the file later – it's not much use with simple text!

5 Click **OK**.

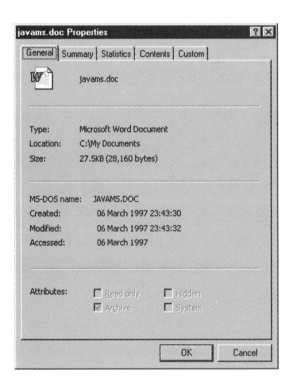

Take note

The General, Summary and Statistics panels can also be opened from within Explorer, but Contents and Custom are only accessible from within the Office filing routines.

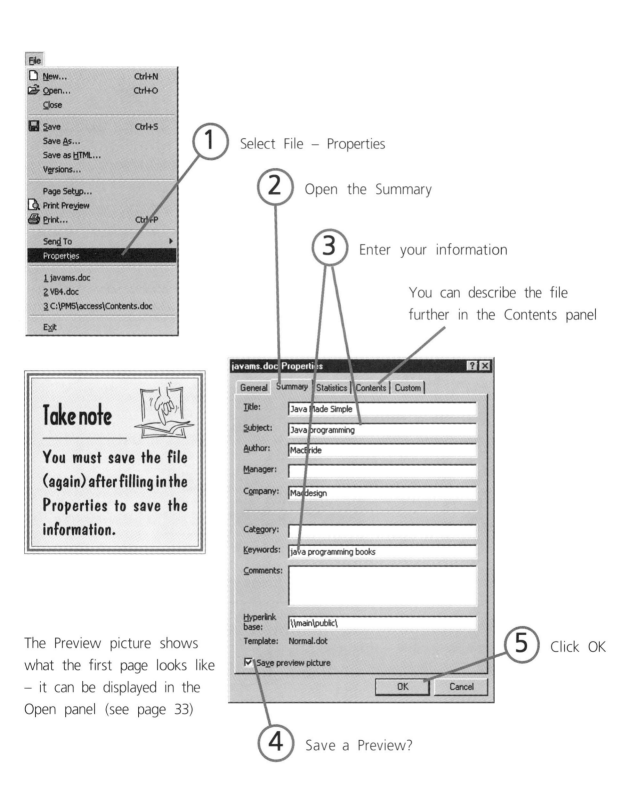

File

New...   Ctrl+N
Open...   Ctrl+O
Close

Save   Ctrl+S
Save As...
Save as HTML...
Versions...

Page Setup...
Print Preview
Print...   Ctrl+P

Send To   ▶
Properties

1 javams.doc
2 VB4.doc
3 C:\PM5\access\Contents.doc

Exit

① Select File – Properties

② Open the Summary

③ Enter your information

You can describe the file further in the Contents panel

Take note

You must save the file (again) after filling in the Properties to save the information.

javams.doc Properties   ? ✕

General | Summary | Statistics | Contents | Custom |

Title: Java Made Simple
Subject: Java programming
Author: MacBride
Manager:
Company: Maddesign

Category:
Keywords: java programming books
Comments:

Hyperlink base: \\main\public\
Template: Normal.dot

☑ Save preview picture

                              OK   Cancel

The Preview picture shows what the first page looks like – it can be displayed in the Open panel (see page 33)

⑤ Click OK

④ Save a Preview?

41

Printing

Because of their different natures, the Office applications vary in their printing routines.

- Word documents are page-based from the start, leading to a simple transition from screen to paper.

- Excel spreadsheets are of indefinite size and highly variable layout. The printout may fit on a single page or be spread across many. To get a good-looking printout you may have to adjust the orientation of the paper, the scale of the print and other aspects.

- PowerPoint is based around slides and handouts, and works to formal layouts. This leaves little room for variation in output to screen or to paper.

Basic steps

- ❑ **Instant print**

- **1** Click 🖨.

- ❑ **Controlled printing**

- **2** In Excel, use **File – Print Area** to select the block of cells to print.

- **3** Open the **File** menu and select **Print**.

- **4** Change the **Printer Name** if necessary.

- **5** Set the **range** of pages or slides to print.

- **6** Set the number of copies.

- **7** Click **OK**.

Take note

These steps are for printing an open document.

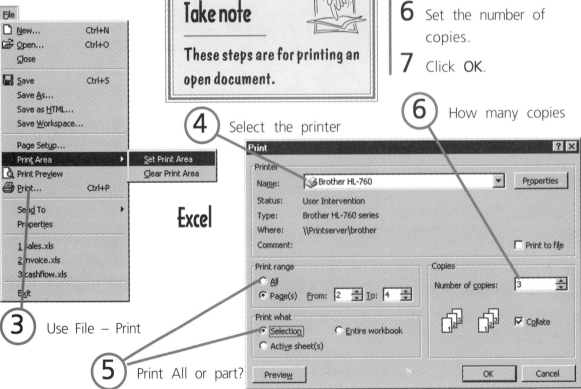

④ Select the printer

⑥ How many copies

③ Use File – Print

Excel

⑤ Print All or part?

PowerPoint

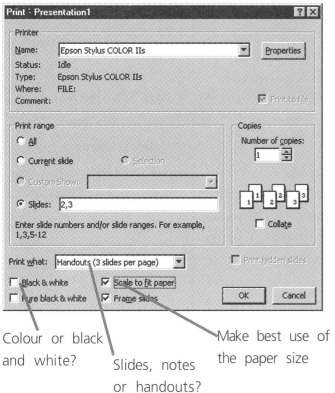

Click **Properties** to set the paper-handling, dots per inch resolution, and other aspects of the printer.

Tip

If you have a problem, the first thing to check is that the printer is on and is loaded with paper!

Colour or black and white?

Slides, notes or handouts?

Make best use of the paper size

Word

A Word document has several additional parts, some of which are only of interest to its author

Take note

If you are printing multiple copies, turning on the Collate option will save you sorting the pages, but will make printing much slower as each copy has to be output separately.

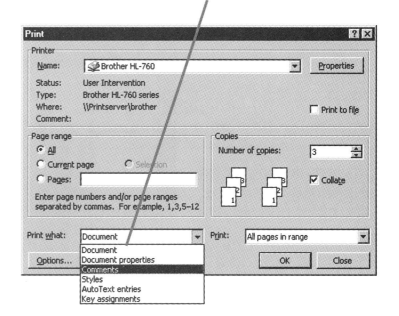

Print Preview

The Preview routines are there not just so that you can *see* how the whole document will look when printed out on separate sheets of paper. They are also there so that you can *change* how it will look. The Excel and Word preview tools are different because there are different kinds of adjustments to make.

Excel

Spreadsheets are usually designed as a whole with the layout and size of blocks of data determined by the data itself. To output them to paper, they must be cut into sections. The odds are that some pages will have odd bits of data that have been sliced off their main blocks on other pages. There are two adjustments that might solve the problem – changing the [Margins] and scaling the whole sheet up or down (done from the [Setup...] button). If neither of these work, you will have to do a major redesign!

Tip

Get into the habit of previewing before you print. It will save paper, ink and time.

Try these for a better fit

Back to the editing screen

'Next' may mean the page below the last, or the one at the top of the next strip

Zoom in to check details

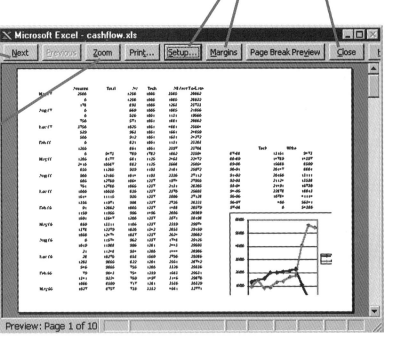

Word

When previewing a Word document, you may want to adjust font sizes, line spacing or the size and position of objects to get a better balanced page. You can do this. All the normal menu commands are available and extra toolbars can be added.

Ruler (on/ off)

Shrink to fit

Full screen (removes frame and menu bar)

Multiple pages

Zoom level

One page

Print

Magnifier (turn off to get editing pointer)

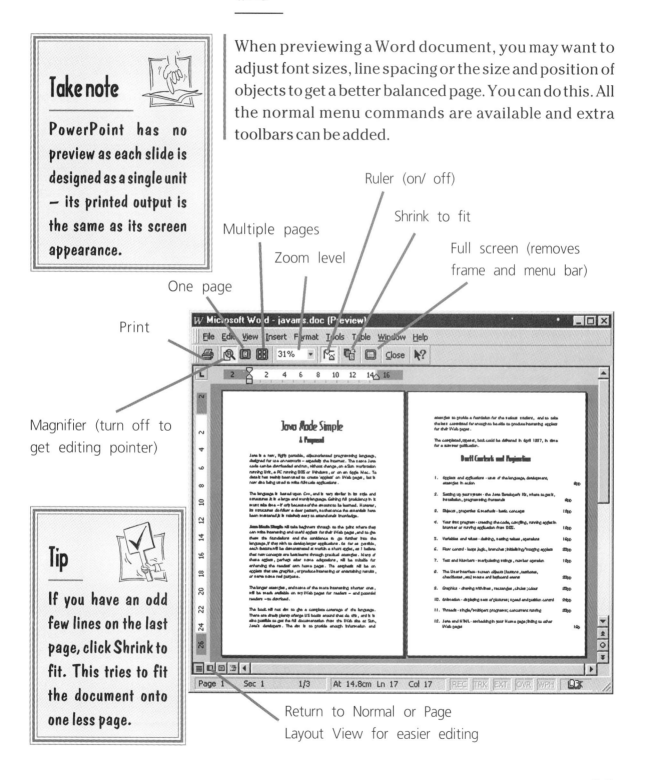

Return to Normal or Page Layout View for easier editing

Page setup

It is always worth checking the Page setup before you print – especially if you are working from a Template, which may well have been designed for different paper or slide sizes to the ones you use.

Basic steps

1 Open the **File** menu and select **Page setup**.

2 In Excel go to the **Paper** panel, in Word go to **Paper Size**.

3 Check the **Orientation** – *Portrait* or *Landscape*. In Powerpoint this may be different for **Slides** and **Notes**.

4 Select a **Paper size** from the list.

5 For draft copies, set the **Print quality** to the lowest dpi (dots per inch) value.

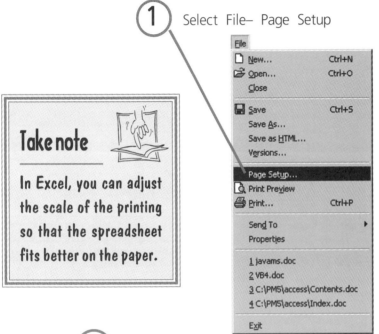

(1) Select File– Page Setup

Take note

In Excel, you can adjust the scale of the printing so that the spreadsheet fits better on the paper.

Excel

(2) Open the Page panel

Headers and Footers are handled from within the document in Word

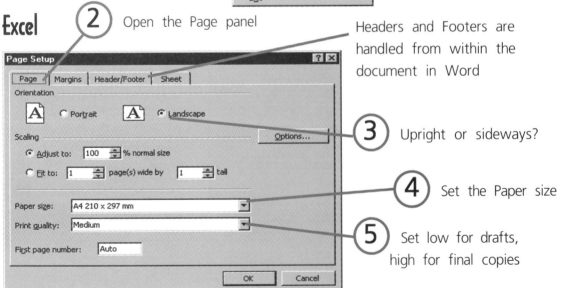

(3) Upright or sideways?

(4) Set the Paper size

(5) Set low for drafts, high for final copies

Setting margins

In Excel or Word, you have a Margins panel where you can adjust the space around the printed area. Sometimes a slight reduction of margins will give you a better printout. There is little more irritating than a couple of odd lines of text or a tiny block of data on a separate sheet.

The Preview gives an idea of the printing area. To see how the actual document will look, use Print Preview.

If the printout is to be bound, set the Gutter to around 1cm and tick Mirror Margins, to give a wider margin on the inside edges.

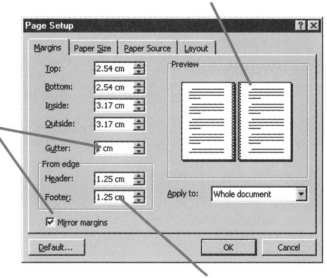

Make sure your margins don't overlap the Header/Footer spaces

③ Upright or sideways?

In **Powerpoint**, the 'Page' can be the screen, 35mm slides or various sizes of paper. You can set different a Orientation for Slides and the other materials.

④ Set the Slide size

Summary

❑ All commands can be accessed through the menus, and all the common ones through the toolbars.

❑ Many of the items on the menus and toolbars are the same in all Office applications.

❑ The **Standard** and **Formatting toolbars** are normally displayed. Other ones can be brought onto the screen as and when they are needed.

❑ Commands can be **added to** or **removed from** menus.

❑ **Files can be opened** from the Shortcut bar or from within applications.

❑ The **File finding** facility helps you to track down files if you have forgotten their names or folders.

❑ There are **templates** and **wizards** available to simplify setting up new documents.

❑ When **saving files** for the first time, you must specify a folder and filename through the Save As dialog box. Resaving simply takes a click on the Save button.

❑ When saving a file, if you save its **Preview**, you will make it easier to find it when you want to open it in the future.

❑ A file's **Properties** panel can hold summary data and a description of the file.

❑ There are some differences in the printing routines, to suit the needs of the different applications.

❑ **Preview** before printing, to check the layout and fit.

❑ Use the **Page setup** dialog box to set margins, paper orientation and print quality.

4 Outlook

Getting organised

Outlook is a personal organiser, and if you are on a local or extended network, it can also be used for arranging meetings of group members.

This is a multi-function system, with its various parts accessed through the **Outlook Bar** down the left side. When you select an item from here, it is displayed in the main window.

Initially, the bar has three groups – you can add more at any point.

The Outlook group

This has five main elements:

- A list of **Contact** names, addresses, phone and fax numbers, with a built-in phone dialler (page 52);

- A **Calendar**, with a reminder facility (page 54);

- A **Tasks** list, for scheduling tasks and monitoring their progress (page 60);

- A **Journal** for logging activites (page 64);

- Notes for jotting down reminders to yourself – these can be stuck anywhere on the desktop.

The elements can be interrelated, linking tasks to contacts or meetings, and contacts to meetings.

The e-mail **Inbox** can also be reached from here, or from...

The Mail group

From here, you can send and receive mail, read messages, create new ones, and organise your storage of old ones. It provides much the same facilities as Microsoft Exchange, or the Mail section in Internet Explorer (or other browser).

Take note

If you like, you can run your working sessions entirely from within Outlook – you can reach your files, programs and every other part of your system from here.

Take note

If you have been using Schedule in Office 95, its contacts lists and other data will be copied into Outlook when it is first set up.

The point of having these facilities within Outlook is that you need the mail for organising meetings over a network. Also, if you do keep Outlook at hand while you work, you do not need to start up another program when you want to send or check your mail. (See page 134 for more.)

The Other group

This provides access to regularly-used folders. You will find links to *My Computer*, and to the *My Documents* and *Favorites* folders – if you still have them on your system. Files can be managed here, just as in Explorer – use it to open, view, print, rename, or send them to another disk or through the mail. You can even run programs from here!

The main display varies with the element being used, and has special options for each type. The screenshot is from Calendar in a Day/Week/ Month view, set here to show a 7-day diary, the month and the Task list.

This deletes any selected item   Display options

Click to open the function

Click to open up the group   Scroll to reach other items in the group

The Contacts list

This is probably the most straightforward part of Outlook to set up. Mind you, it will take a while if you give all the details that it can hold – home and business address, phone and fax, birthdays, spouse, assistant, dog's name....

Basic steps

1 Open **Contacts**.

2 Open the **Contacts** menu and select **New Contact** or click [icon].

3 On the **General** tab, enter the name and other contact details.

4 Switch to other tabs to add more if wanted.

5 Click **Save and Close**.

❑ The new name will be slotted into the list in alphabetical order

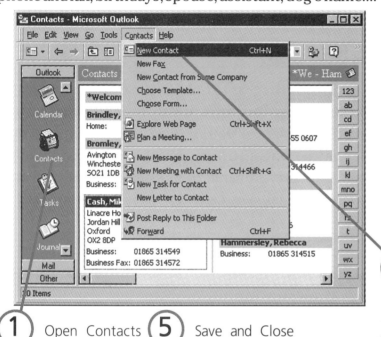

② Use Contacts – New Contact

④ Any other details?

① Open Contacts ⑤ Save and Close

③ Enter details

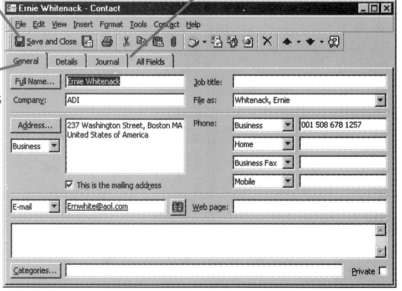

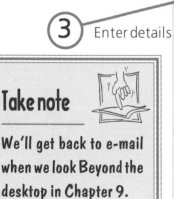

Take note

We'll get back to e-mail when we look Beyond the desktop in Chapter 9.

Basic steps

1 Open **Contacts**.
2 Use the index buttons, if necessary, to get to the right place.
3 Select the person.
4 Click 🕿 or select **Dial from** the **Tools** menu.
5 Click **Start Call**.
6 Lift the phone.
7 When the number rings, click **Talk**.

Phone dialling

If your phone is connected through the PC's modem, you can get Outlook to dial for you.

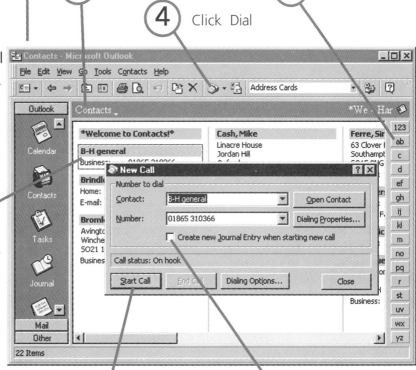

(1) Open Contacts

(2) Use the index

(4) Click Dial

(3) Select the contact

(5) Start the call

Do you want to log the call? (See page 64.)

(7) Click Talk

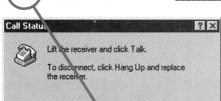

Hang up when you've done

Take note

The dialler's drop-down list lets you repeat the last call, make a New Call to a number that is not in your book, Redial recently used numbers or access your Speed Dial list.

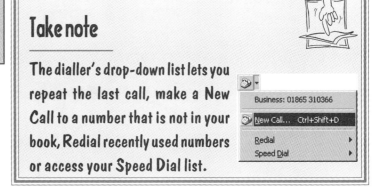

Calendar options

There are optional settings for all aspects of the Outlook system. Many of these can be left at their defaults; some should be looked at when you have got used to Outlook and want to fine-tune it; the Calendar needs early attention.

You need to set the defaults for:

- The pattern of your working week, and working day;
- How long before a meeting you receive a reminder;
- The public holidays for your country.

1 Open **Tools** menu and select **Options...**

2 Switch to the **Calendar** panel.

3 Tick your **working days.**

4 Set your normal **working hours**.

5 Set the **Reminder** notice time.

6 Click **Add Holidays.**

7 Select the country.

8 Click **OK** then close the **Options** window.

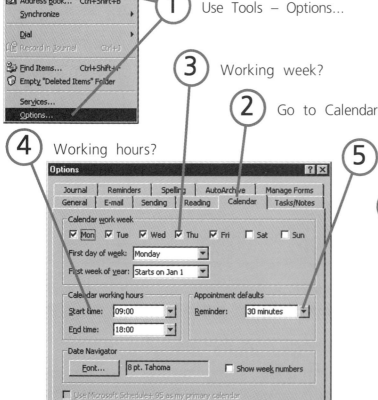

Use Tools – Options...

③ Working week?

② Go to Calendar

④ Working hours?

⑤ Set the Reminder notice

⑦ Select the country

⑧ Click OK

⑥ Click Add Holidays

Basic steps

1 Open the **Calendar** panel.
2 Switch to **1 Day** view.
3 Select the day.
4 Point to the start time and drag highlight to the planned end time.
5 Click 🖼 or select **New Appointment** from the **Calendar** menu.
6 Enter a **Subject**.
7 Enter the **Location**.
8 Click **Save and Close**.

Making a date

A simple appointment can be set up in seconds.

(1) Open Calendar

(2) Click 1 Day

(3) Select the day

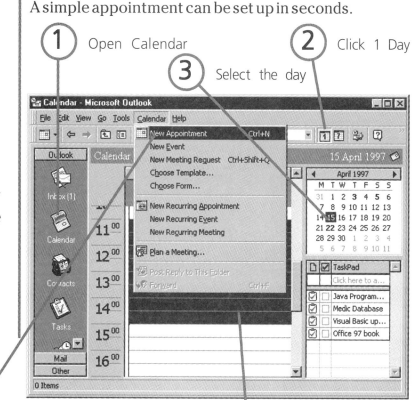

(5) Use Calendar – New Appointment

(4) Highlight the times

(8) Save and Close

(6) Enter a Subject

(7) Enter the Location

Want a reminder? How long before?

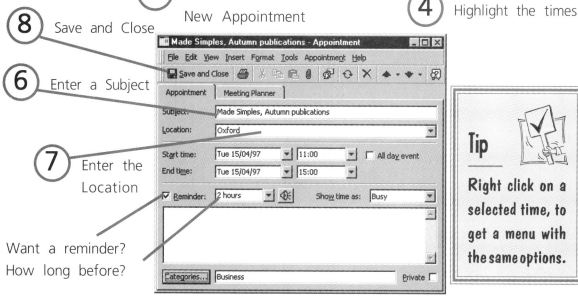

Tip

Right click on a selected time, to get a menu with the same options.

Recurring appointments

If you have a series of regular appointments, you can set them all up in one operation.

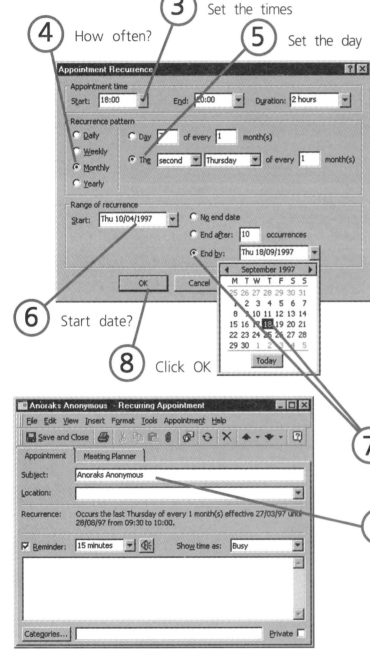

③ Set the times

④ How often?

⑤ Set the day

⑥ Start date?

⑧ Click OK

⑦ End date?

⑨ Add details and save

Basic steps

1 Follow steps 1 to 4 on the previous page to set the day and time of the first of the series.

2 Select **New Recuring Appointment** from the **Calendar** menu.

3 Check the times.

4 In **Recurrence pattern**, set the **frequency**.

5 Set the **Day** (of the week, month or year).

6 Check the **Start** date.

7 Select **No end date**, or **End after** or **End by** and set the limit.

8 Click **OK**.

9 Complete as for a simple appointment.

Arranging meetings

1 Select the day and time as for an appointment (see page 55).

2 Select **New Meeting Request** from the **Calendar** menu.

3 Click the **To:** button.

...continued overleaf

This is probably of most use to people working on a local area network, where each has access to the (public) diary of the others. But, it is also a convenient way to call a meeting with those whom you can contact by fax or e-mail.

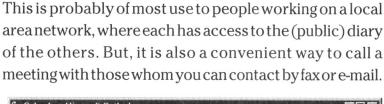

(2) Use Calendar – New Meeting Request

(3) Click To:

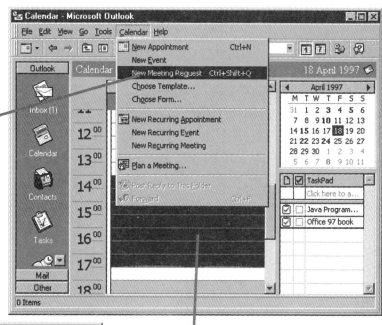

(1) Set the date and time

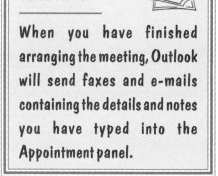

Take note

When you have finished arranging the meeting, Outlook will send faxes and e-mails containing the details and notes you have typed into the Appointment panel.

Basic steps

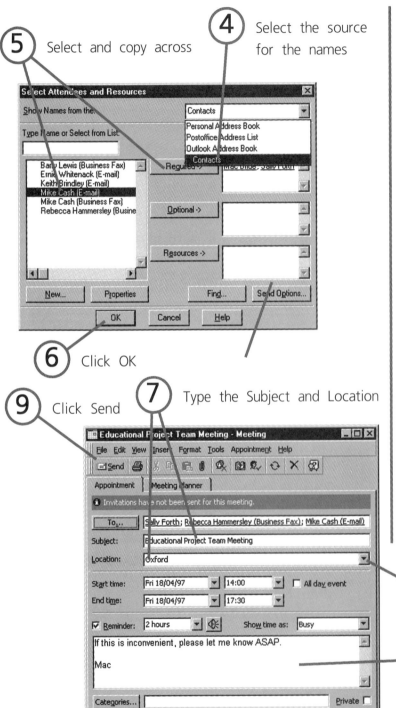

5 Select and copy across

4 Select the source for the names

6 Click OK

9 Click Send

7 Type the Subject and Location

8 Add a message

Previously-used locations can be picked from the drop-down list

4 Open the Show Names from list and select the source – **Post Office Address book** for the local area network and probably **Contacts** for external mail and fax.

5 Select the attendees who are **Required** or **Optional**, or will supply **Resources**, and click the buttons to copy them to the appropriate panes.

6 Click **OK**.

7 Back at the **Appointment** panel, type the **Subject** and **Location**.

8 Type any message that you want to add to the meeting notice.

9 Click **Send**.

Basic steps

1 If you have closed the Appointment panel, double-click on the time to re-open it.

2 Switch to the **Meeting Planner** panel.

3 Check for clashes – you can only do this for people on your local network.

❏ **To adjust the time**

4 Drag the start or end line for minor adjustments.

or

5 Click `<< AutoPick >>`, heading backwards or forwards to let Outlook find the next free time for all attendees.

6 Type a message on the Appointments panel, if needed.

7 Click **Send**, or if you have already sent a request, **Send Update**.

The Meeting Planner

Where the other attendees are on your local area network – and are all using Outlook's Calendar to plan their time – you can check their availability. On the Meeting Planner panel, you can see who is busy when, and can rearrange your meeting time if necessary.

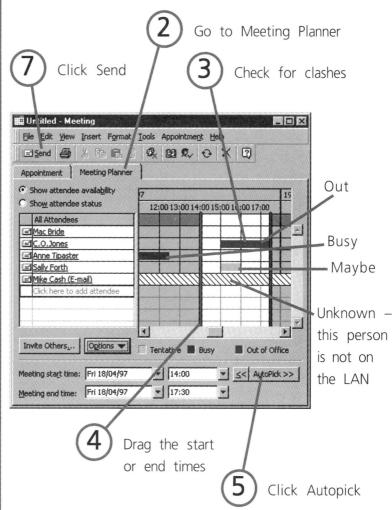

② Go to Meeting Planner

⑦ Click Send

③ Check for clashes

Out

Busy

Maybe

Unknown – this person is not on the LAN

④ Drag the start or end times

⑤ Click Autopick

Tasks

Use the Tasks module to keep track of your current and scheduled tasks. For each task you can record:

● The start and due dates;

● The percentage complete;

● The status and priority;

● The *Categories*–this can be just a way of keeping the same kinds of jobs together, or it can be a way of organising multi-part projects and monitoring the progress of the component tasks.

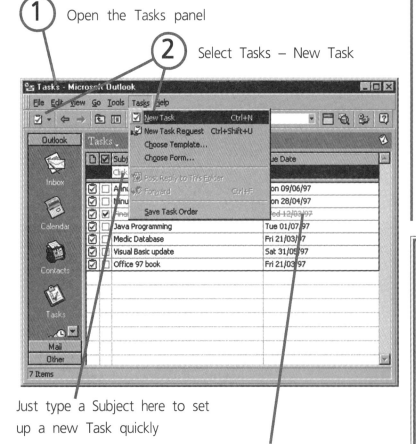

Open the Tasks panel

Select Tasks – New Task

Just type a Subject here to set up a new Task quickly

Completed tasks are crossed off – use ☒ to delete them when the records are no longer needed.

1 Open the **Tasks** panel.

2 Pull down the **Tasks** menu and select **New Task** or click ☑.

3 Type a **Subject**.

4 Set the **Due date** and **Start date**, if relevant.

5 Select the **Status** from the drop-down list.

6 Click ⬚Categories...⬚.

7 Select one or more **Categories**.

8 Click **OK**.

9 Switch to the **Status** tab and add any known details.

10 Click **Save and Close**.

Take note

If you don't want to enter the details for a new task, type the Subject into the 'Click here to add a new task' slot. Double-click to open the Task panel, and add or edit the details later.

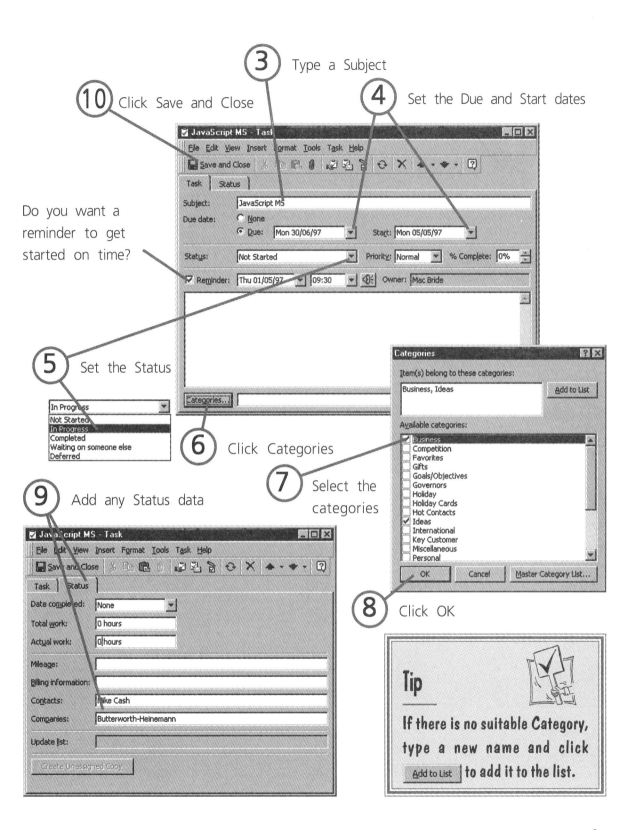

③ Type a Subject

⑩ Click Save and Close

④ Set the Due and Start dates

Do you want a reminder to get started on time?

⑤ Set the Status

⑥ Click Categories

⑦ Select the categories

⑧ Click OK

⑨ Add any Status data

Tip

If there is no suitable Category, type a new name and click Add to List to add it to the list.

61

Different views

If you have a lot of jobs in your task list, the normal display can make it difficult to find the one you want, or to compare one with another. Outlook offers ten ways to organise and view your tasks.

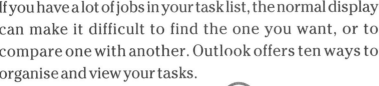

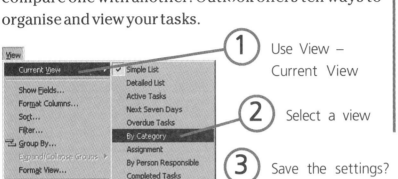

① Use View – Current View

② Select a view

③ Save the settings?

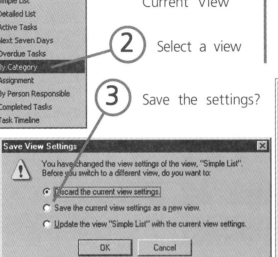

1 From the **View** menu, select **Current View**.

2 Select a view.

3 If you have adjusted the display, you can **Save** or **Discard** the settings – make your choice.

Take note

There are alternative Views in all parts of Outlook. The Category View is available in all.

Click the column heading to sort the tasks in order of that heading
- △ Ascending order
- ▽ Descending order

The Categories act like folders

Click on ⊞ to open a category

Click on ⊟ to close

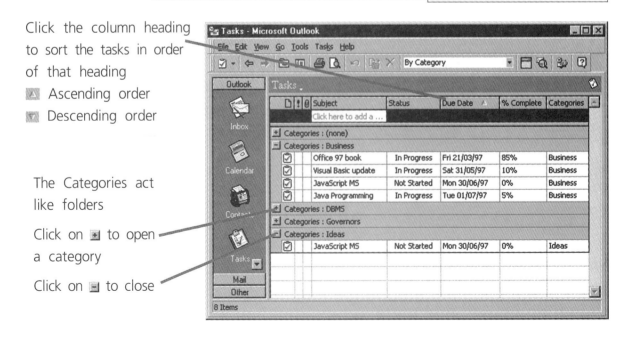

Basic steps

1 From the **View** menu, select **Show Fields...**

2 Select fields from the list of all fields in the left pane and click **Add** to show them.

3 Select from the current field list in the right pane and click **Remove** to simplify the display.

4 Use **Move Up** and **Move Down** to adjust the order.

5 Click **OK**.

You can use the Folder list instead of the Outlook bar to switch between folders

Adjusting the view

Outlook gives you many options for adjusting the view. Choosing which fields to show is worth investigating.

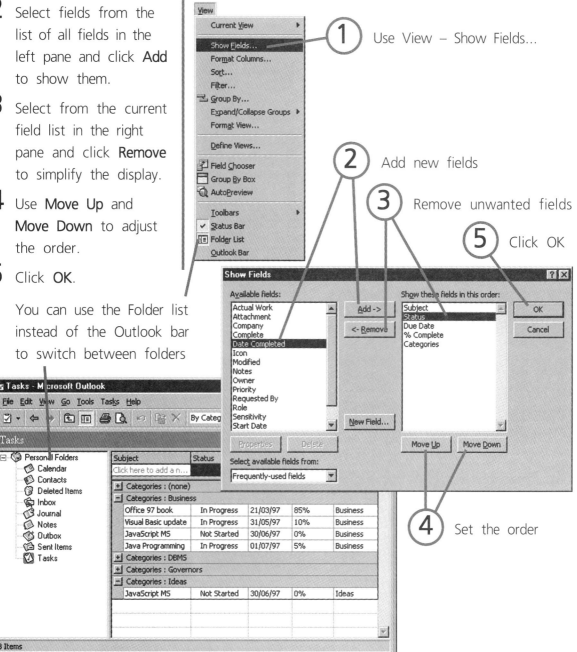

① Use View – Show Fields...

② Add new fields

③ Remove unwanted fields

⑤ Click OK

④ Set the order

The Journal

If you need to keep a record of the work you have done – either for your own later reference, or for billing purposes – have a look at the Journal. You can create a Journal entry at any time, though the simplest approach is to set it up to log automatically those activities that you normally need to record. Unwanted entries are easily removed.

Basic steps

- ❑ **Automatic logging**

1 Open the **Tools** menu and select **Options**.

2 Switch to **Journal**.

3 Tick those **items**, **contacts** and **files** that you want logging.

4 Click **OK**.

- ❑ **Single entry**

5 From the **New ...** menu select **Journal Entry**.

6 Type the **Subject**.

7 Select an **Entry type**.

8 Add a note.

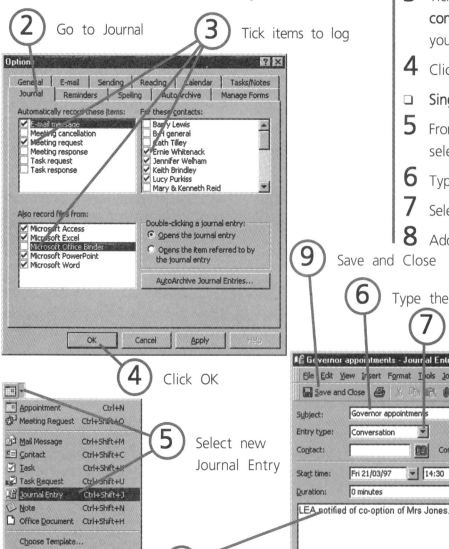

② Go to Journal ③ Tick items to log

④ Click OK

⑤ Select new Journal Entry

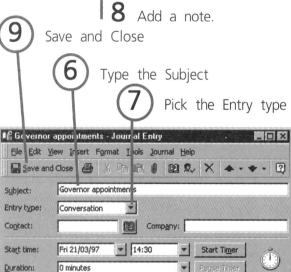

⑨ Save and Close

⑥ Type the Subject

⑦ Pick the Entry type

⑧ Add a note

Basic steps

1 Open the **Journal** panel.

2 Select a **View**. *By type* and *Last Seven Days* are useful views.

3 Click ⊞ to open a group.

4 Right-click on an entry for the short menu.

5 Select **Open Journal Entry** to read or edit the entry.

Reading the journal

① Open the Journal

② Select a View

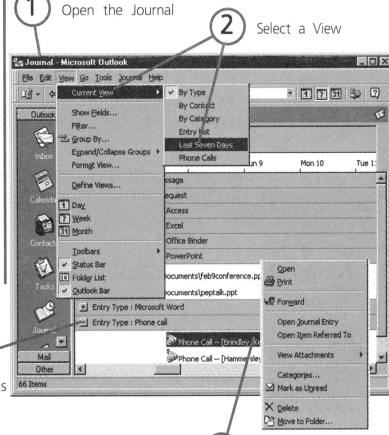

③ Open groups as required

④ Right-click an entry for its menu

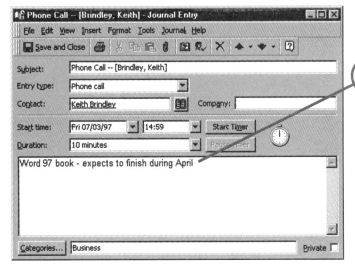

⑤ Open the Entry for editing

Tip

You can use Open to open a logged file in its application.

Notes

If you are the sort of person who writes notes to yourself, here is an alternative to having Post-Its™ stuck to the side of your monitor. Outlook Notes save paper, and they don't drop off! You can keep them in the Notes folder, or stick them anywhere on your desktop – though not onto documents.

1 Open the **Notes** panel.

2 Open the **Note** menu and select **New Note** or click 🖼.

3 Type your note – if you put a title in the top line, it will stand out more in the folder.

4 Drag the note onto the desktop, if wanted.

5 Click ⊠ to close the note – it will be saved.

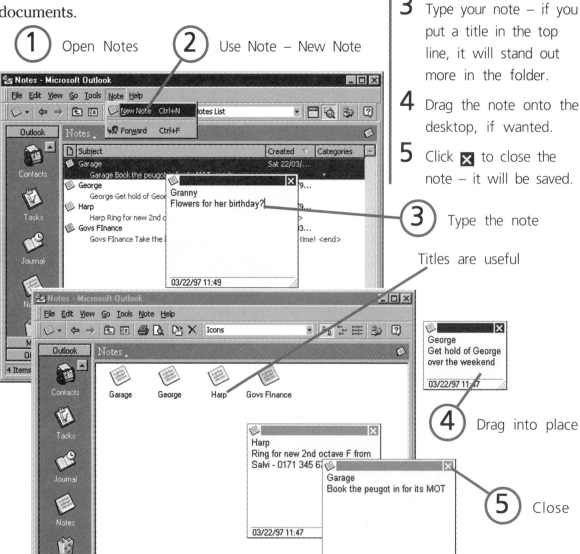

① Open Notes ② Use Note – New Note

③ Type the note

Titles are useful

④ Drag into place

⑤ Close

Reminders

We have seen that you can set reminders for appointments and tasks. Those for appointments appear 15 minutes (or however long you chose) before the event; reminders for tasks appear at a set time (normally the start) of the day.

If Office Assistant is running, it gives the reminder; if not, a standard message box is used. The options are the same either way.

- Click **Dismiss** to clear the reminder;
- Set the delay and click **Postpone** for a further reminder;
- Use **Open Item** to read the event or task panel.

OK, I'll get my coat

What am I supposed to be doing?

This job is running late – give me a few more days!

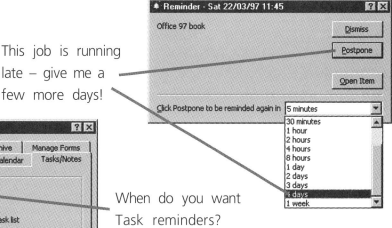

When do you want Task reminders?

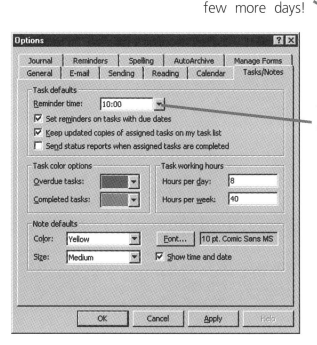

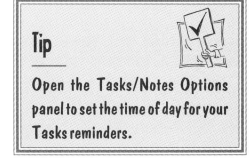

Tip

Open the Tasks/Notes Options panel to set the time of day for your Tasks reminders.

Summary

❑ Outlook is a **personal** and **workgroup organizer** in which you can store contacts, appointments and lists of tasks.

❑ The **Contacts list** can be used to record very complete details of your contacts.

❑ You can **dial phone numbers** in your Contacts list by clicking the dialler button.

❑ Most of the **Options** can be left at their defaults, but you should set up the Calendar options, and those for the Journal if you are going to use this.

❑ When adding **appointments**, you can set them to **recur** weekly, monthly or at any fixed interval.

❑ **Reminders** can be set for any time before an appointment.

❑ You can use Outlook to **arrange meetings** with others on your network, or accessible by fax or e-mail.

❑ The **Task list** can be used to schedule activities and to record progress on them. Reminders can be set for time-limited tasks.

❑ All Outlook panels have a choice of **Views**. Use them to focus on different aspects of your work.

❑ The **Journal** can log your activities automatically, and entries can also be made at any time.

❑ You need never forget anything if you set **Reminders** for you appointments and tasks, and stick **Notes** about other things on your Desktop.

Take note

The Mail-handling aspects of Outlook are covered in Chapter 9, Beyond the desktop.

5 Working with text

Selecting text

There are essentially two approaches to formatting text.

● You can set the style, type the text, then turn the style off, or set a new style.

● Or you can type in your text, then go back over it, selecting blocks and formatting them.

It is generally simplest to get the text typed first and format it to suit later – but before you can format it, you must select it.

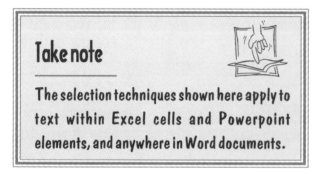

Take note

The selection techniques shown here apply to text within Excel cells and Powerpoint elements, and anywhere in Word documents.

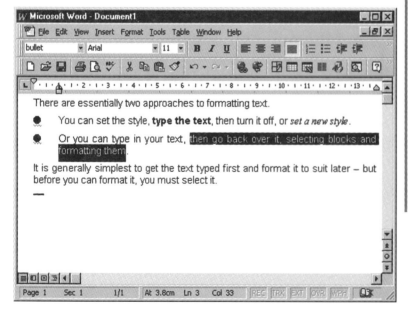

❑ **With a mouse**

1 Point to the start of the text to be selected.

2 Hold the left mouse button down and drag to the last character.

3 Release the mouse button.

❑ **Click tricks**

1 Place the I-beam in a word.

2 Double-click the left button to select the word.

or

3 Triple-click to select the whole paragraph.

❑ **With the [Shift] key**

1 Move the I-beam to the first character.

2 Hold down **[Shift]** and use the arrow keys to move the I-beam to the last character.

3 Release **[Shift]**.

Click here to select
the whole sheet

Select whole columns by
selecting their letters

Select whole rows
by selecting their
numbers

You can select and
format a block
within a cell

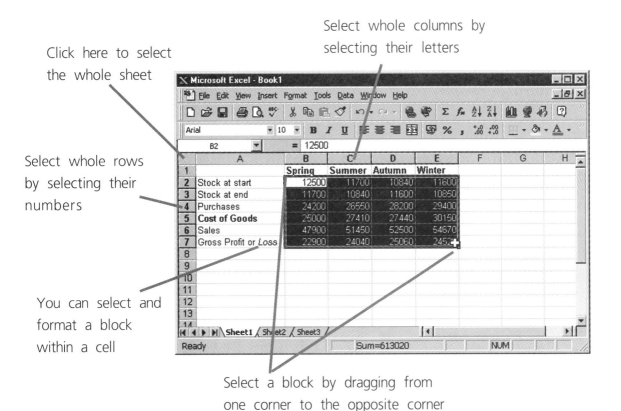

Select a block by dragging from
one corner to the opposite corner

To select one or
more elements,
drag an outline to
enclose them

Blocks within
the text can be
selected in the
usual ways

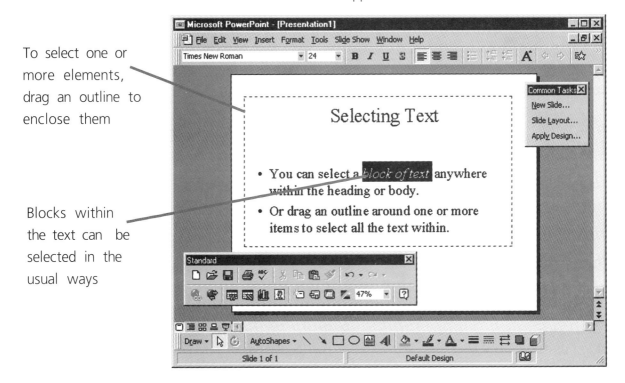

Fonts

The Formatting Toolbars

These hold all the tools you need for everyday work. There are minor differences between the applications, reflecting their different requirements.

Basic steps

1 Select the text.

2 Click the Toolbar buttons to set fonts and styles.

or

3 Right click within the selected area to open the short menu.

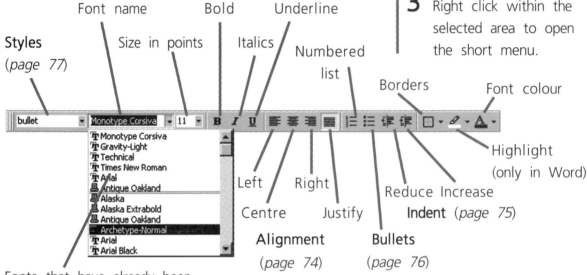

Styles (*page 77*)

Font name

Size in points

Bold

Italics

Underline

Numbered list

Borders

Font colour

Left

Centre

Right

Justify

Highlight (only in Word)

Reduce Increase

Indent (*page 75*)

Alignment (*page 74*)

Bullets (*page 76*)

Fonts that have already been used in the document are listed at the top for easy re-use.

The Fonts dialog box

There will be times when the tolbars are not enough and you need to turn to the Fonts dialog box. Use this when you want to:

- set $_{subscript,}$ ^{superscript}, and other effects;
- convert headings to FULL or SMALL CAPITALS;
- check the suitability of a **new font;**
- use coloured text.

Tip

Some fonts are larger or heavier than others of the same size and style. That's why you should always choose your font before changing the settings.

4 Select **Font** (**Format cells** in Excel).

5 Switch to the **Font** panel if it is not already open.

6 If you are going to change the font, *do this first.*

7 Set other effects as required, checking the appearance in the Preview pane.

8 Click **OK**.

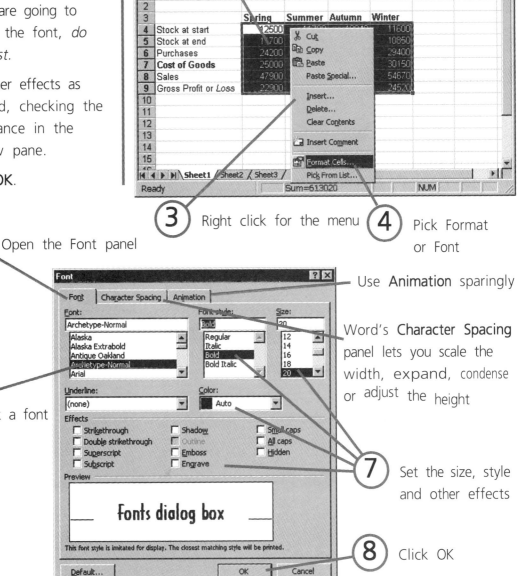

① Select the text

② Use the Toolbar buttons

③ Right click for the menu

④ Pick Format or Font

⑤ Open the Font panel

⑥ Pick a font

⑦ Set the size, style and other effects

⑧ Click OK

Use **Animation** sparingly

Word's **Character Spacing** panel lets you scale the width, expand, condense or adjust the height

Alignment and Indents

Alignment

This refers to how text fits against the margins (or the edges of Excel cells). Four options are always available: Left, Right, Centre and Justify (aligned to both margins)

Excel also has other options to handle headings. You can:

● centre the text from one cell across a range of cells, perhaps to give a table a heading;

● set column labels vertical or at an angle.

Text centred across columns A to E

Select the cells

Click to centre

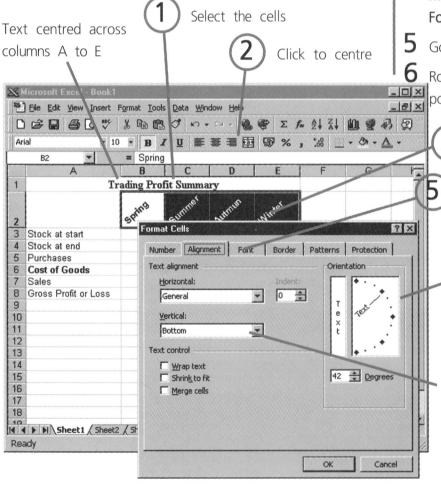

❑ **Centred headings**

1 Select the cells that the text is to be centred in.

2 Click 🔳 – **Centre Across Columns**.

❑ **Angled text**

3 Select the cells

4 Right click for the menu and select **Format Cells..**

5 Go to **Alignment**.

6 Rotate the **Text** — pointer as desired

3 Select the cells

5 Open Alignment

6 Rotate the pointer

Text can also be aligned *Vertically* – to the top, bottom or centre of the row

Basic steps

1 Select the text
2 Click ⊞ (Word) or ⇨ (PowerPoint) to indent

or

3 Click ⊞ (Word) or ⇦ (Powerpoint) to pull back out

Indents

Indents set the distance from the edge of the page margins, or of the cells in Excel. In Word and PowerPoint, they can also be used to create a structure.

Indenting is simplest with the buttons – each click pushes the text in (or out) 5mm.

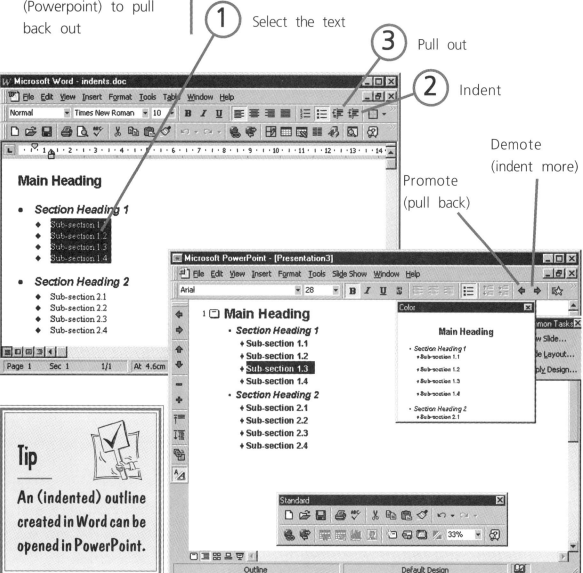

① Select the text

③ Pull out

② Indent

Demote (indent more)

Promote (pull back)

Tip

An (indented) outline created in Word can be opened in PowerPoint.

Bullets

In Word, you can quickly add numbers or bullets to each item in a list by clicking ▤ or ▤. For finer control, use Format – Bullets and Numbering.

Basic steps

1 Select the whole list.

2 Open the **Format** menu and select **Bullets and Numbering**.

3 Select the basic style.

4 Click **Customize...**

5 Pick a bullet, or click **Bullet...** for more.

6 Select a font – try *Symbol* or *Wingdings*.

7 Hold the mouse button down for a close up – double-click to select.

③ Set the basic style

④ Click Customize

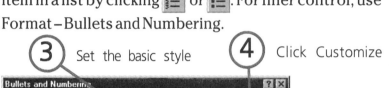

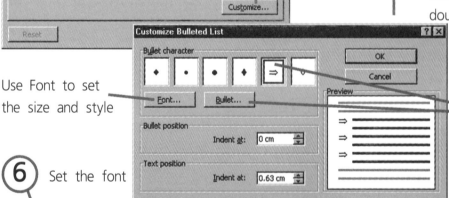

Use Font to set the size and style

⑤ Pick a bullet

⑥ Set the font

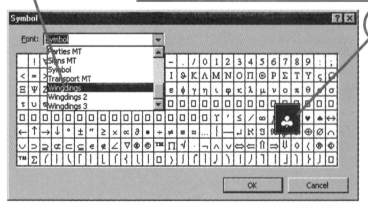

⑦ Double-click to select

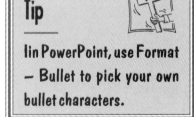

Tip

In PowerPoint, use Format – Bullet to pick your own bullet characters.

76

Basic steps

- ❏ **Excel – applying a style**

1 Select the text or cells.

2 Open the **Format** menu and select **Style...**

3 At the **Style** dialog box, select one from the **Style name** list.

4 Click **OK**.

- ❏ **Creating a new style**

5 Type in a **Style Name**.

6 Click [Modify...].

7 Work through the panels, editing the settings.

8 Click **OK**.

9 Clear the checkboxes for aspects that you do not want to format.

10 Click [Add].

Tip

To modify an existing style, select it from the list and follow steps 6–9 only.

A *style* is a combination of font, size, alignment and indent options. Word and Excel both come with a range of pre-defined styles, and you can modify these or add your own to the sets. Applying a style is a matter of a couple of clicks; creating a new style is almost as simple.

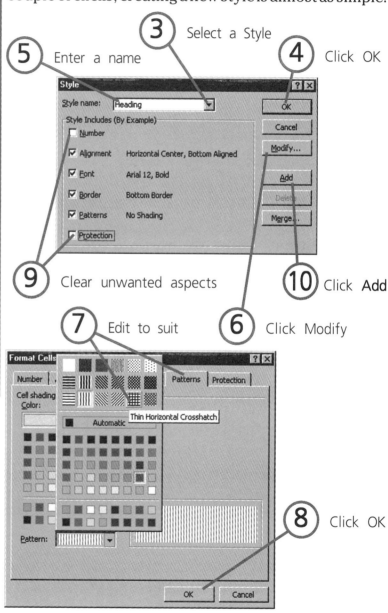

③ Select a Style

⑤ Enter a name

④ Click OK

⑨ Clear unwanted aspects

⑩ Click **Add**

⑦ Edit to suit

⑥ Click Modify

⑧ Click OK

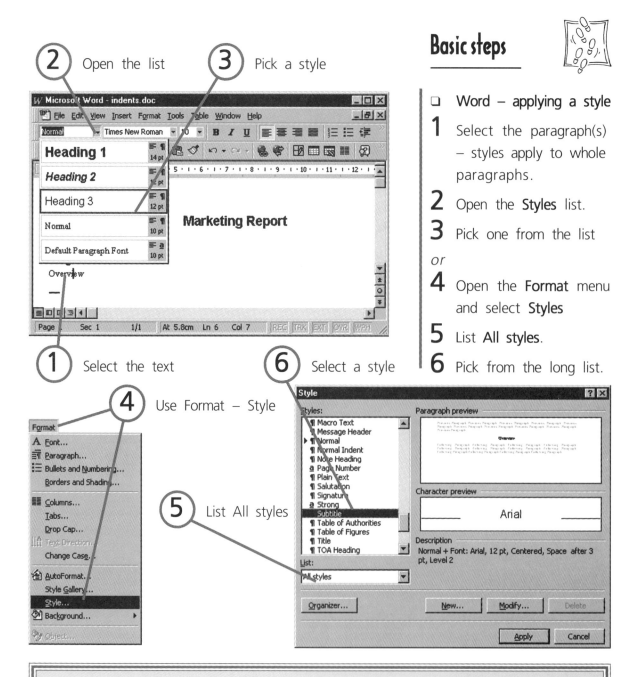

Basic steps

- ❏ **Word – applying a style**

1 Select the paragraph(s) – styles apply to whole paragraphs.

2 Open the **Styles** list.

3 Pick one from the list

or

4 Open the **Format** menu and select **Styles**

5 List **All styles**.

6 Pick from the long list.

Take note

Word has a huge set of styles – from tables of contents to multiple levels of index, with headings, captions and body styles in between. Excel has a limited set, geared to presentation of numbers.

❑ **Word – modifying a style**

1 At the **Style** dialog box, pick the style.

2 Click [Modify...].

3 Click [Format ▼].

4 Select an aspect and edit the settings.

5 Repeat 3 and 4 as necessary.

6 Click **OK**, and **Apply** at the **Style** dialog box.

❑ **Creating a style**

7 At the **Style** dialog box, click [New...].

8 Type in a **Name** then follow steps 3 to 6.

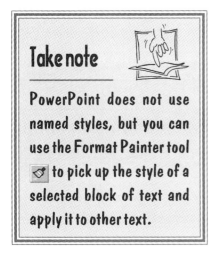

Take note

PowerPoint does not use named styles, but you can use the Format Painter tool ✎ to pick up the style of a selected block of text and apply it to other text.

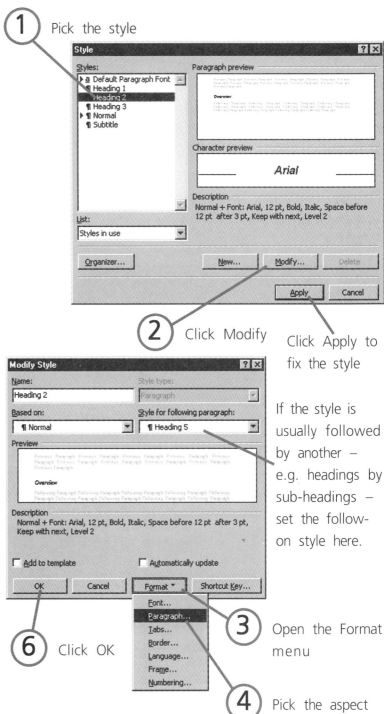

① Pick the style

② Click Modify

Click Apply to fix the style

If the style is usually followed by another – e.g. headings by sub-headings – set the follow-on style here.

⑥ Click OK

③ Open the Format menu

④ Pick the aspect

Autoformats

When word-processors added facilities for fancy fonts and layouts, productivity in many offices took a great leap *backwards*. Instead of simply typing and printing their documents, people spent time – often too much – prettying them up. Not enough people asked themselves if it was really worth the effort. The trouble is, if you want your documents to look 'professional', plain typing will no longer do. But don't worry, here's a great leap forward. The Autoformats in Word and Excel give you attractive documents *instantly*.

Basic steps

❑ **Word Autoformat**

1 Open the **Format** menu and select **Autoformat**.

2 Select **Autoformat and review**, then click **OK**.

3 When you get the **Formatting completed** message, click
[Style Gallery...].

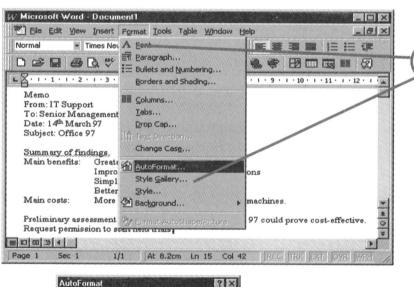

Select Format – AutoFormat...

Accept changes

Open the Style Gallery

Review the changes

Select Review and click OK

Basic steps

4 At the **Style Gallery**, select a style, checking it in the preview screen.

5 Click **OK** when you find one you like.

6 Click [Review Changes...].

7 Use the Find buttons to work through the changes and [Reject] any you don't like.

8 Click [Cancel] to end the review.

9 Click [Accept All].

---

④ Check out the Styles

Style Gallery

Template: nos\Elegant Memo.dot

(current)
Contemporary Lett
Contemporary Mer
Contemporary Rep
ebook
ebook1
Elegant Letter
Elegant Memo
Elegant Report
HTML
letter
More Cool Stuff
More Templates ar
NORMAL
Professional Letter
Professional Memo
Professional Repor

Preview
● Document
○ Example
○ Style samples

Preview of: Memo

> MEMO
>
> From: IT Support
> To: Senior Management Team
> Date: 14th March 97
> Subject: Office 97
>
> Summary of findings
>
> Main benefits: Greater ease of use
> Improved integration between applications
> Simple access to the Internet
> Better organiser software
> Main costs: More memory will be needed on some machines.
>
> Preliminary assessment suggests that upgrading to Office 97 could prove cost-effective.
>
> Request permission to start field trials.

[OK] [Cancel]

⑤ Click OK

The new format is shown here

Microsoft Word - memo.doc

File Edit View Insert Format Tools Table Window Help

Document Labe ▾ Garamond ▾ 9 ▾ **B** *I* U

MEMO

From: IT Support¶
To: Senior Management Team¶
Date: 14th March 97¶
Subject: Office 97¶
¶
Summary of
Main benefit

Review AutoFormat Changes

Changes
Applied style Document Label.

[← Find]
[⇨ Find]

[Reject] [Hide Marks] [Undo] [Cancel]

Main costs:
¶
Preliminary assessment suggests that upgrading to Office 97 could prove cost-eff
Request permission to start field trials.¶

Page 1   Sec 1   1/1   At 2.5cm   Ln 1   Col 1   REC TRK EXT OVR WPH

⑦ Check the changes

⑧ Cancel to end

Tip

If you don't have many styles, run **Add/Remove Office 97** programs and add more from the Word Template options.

AutoFormat Options

These Word options can be reached using the **File – AutoFormat** command. On the **AutoFormat** tab, select those items that you want the formatting to cover. If in doubt, leave all the options on. Later you can turn off those which do not prove to be useful.

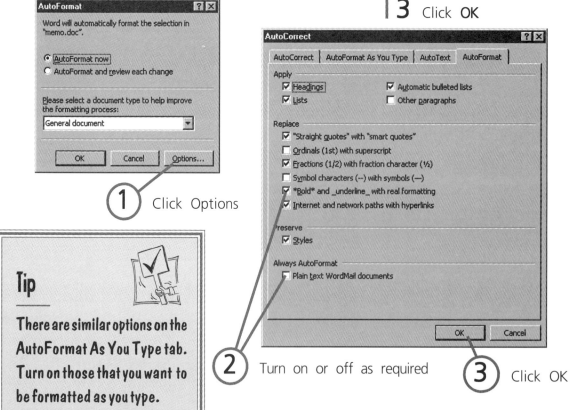

① Click Options

② Turn on or off as required

③ Click OK

Tip

There are similar options on the AutoFormat As You Type tab. Turn on those that you want to be formatted as you type.

Excel AutoFormat

Excel has a wide range of ready-made formats for tables of data. Select the table, give the Format – AutoFormat command and select a style from the list.

82

Basic steps

1 At the **AutoFormat** dialog box, click Options....

2 Go to **AutoCorrect**.

3 Put a tick by those items that you want Word to correct.

❑ **Adding to the list**

4 In the document, type the text correctly and select it.

5 Open the **AutoFormat** dialog box and go to **AutoCorrect**.

6 Click **Plain Text**.

7 Enter the error or a character combination into the **Replace** slot.

8 Click Add.

Don't confuse this with the spell checker. There are similarities, in that both correct typing, but AutoCorrect performs a one-for-one substitution from a limited list, rather than checking against a large dictionary. Use it to:

● correct common transpositions – **teh** into **the;**

● correct common misspellings – **acheive** into **achieve;**

● call up special characters – type **(c)** and AutoCorrect swaps it for ©.

You can add your own common 'typos' or substitutions to the list if they are not already there.

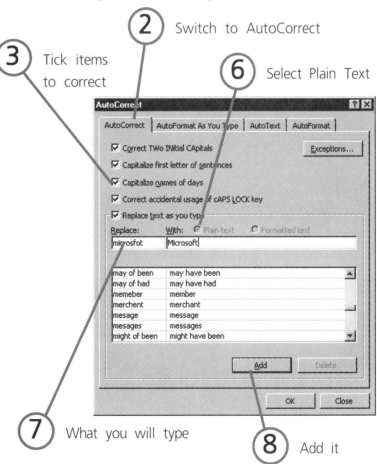

② Switch to AutoCorrect

③ Tick items to correct

⑥ Select Plain Text

⑦ What you will type

⑧ Add it

Tip

If you want the substituted text to always be formatted in a certain way, format it first, and use the Formatted text option in Autocorrect.

Exceptions for Capitalising

Word's version of AutoCorrect also checks that the first letters of sentences are capitals. As a sentence is defined as something that comes after a full stop, abbreviations can create problems. The solution is to have a list of abbreviations and not capitalise words that follow them. You can add to this list.

1 Open the **AutoCorrect** dialog box and click `Exceptions...`.

2 Switch to the **First Letter** panel.

3 Type your new abbreviation in the **Don't Capitalize After** slot.

4 Click `Add`.

Are the other Capital rules right for you?

① Click Exceptions

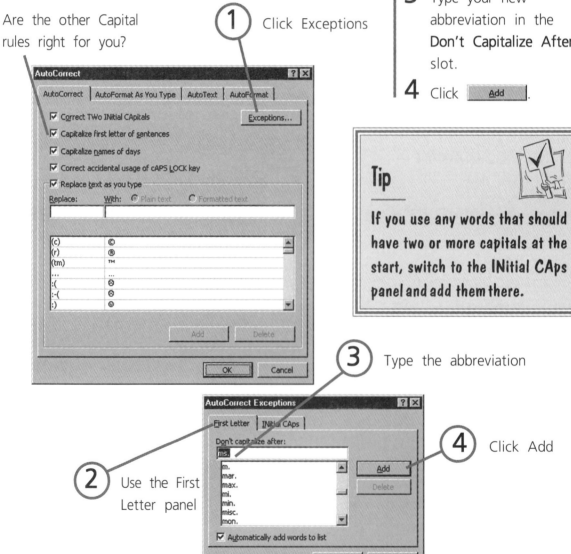

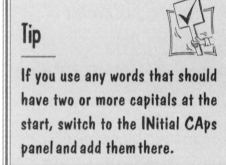

② Use the First Letter panel

③ Type the abbreviation

④ Click Add

Tip

If you use any words that should have two or more capitals at the start, switch to the INitial CAps panel and add them there.

Basic steps

Undo/Redo

- ❏ Undoing one action

1 Click the arrow on the Undo button 🔙.

- ❏ Undoing one action

2 Open the list from the Undo button 🔙.

3 Point down the list to highlight all the actions that you want to undo.

4 Click the left mouse button.

Undo

In the old days, you were lucky if your software allowed you to undo a mistake. With the Office applications you can go back and undo a whole string of actions. This doesn't just protect you from the results of hasty decisions or self-willed mice, it gives you a freedom to experiment. You can do major editing or reformatting, and if at the end you preferred things how they were, you can undo your way back to it.

Redo

This is the undo-undo button! If you undid too much, use this to put it back again. Use it for the last action, or a whole sequence, exactly as with Undo.

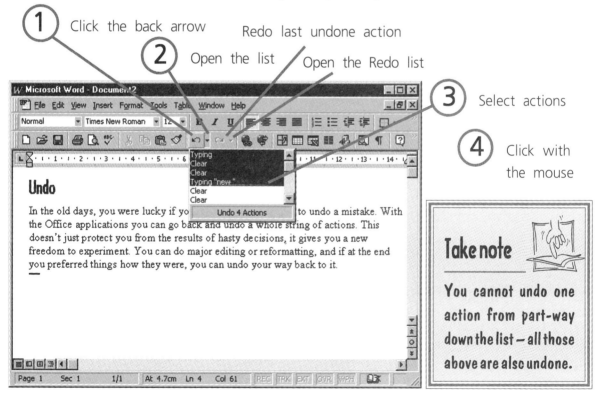

① Click the back arrow

② Open the list

Redo last undone action

Open the Redo list

③ Select actions

④ Click with the mouse

Take note

You cannot undo one action from part-way down the list – all those above are also undone.

Spelling

The main spell checking system is available in all Office applications. There is a good dictionary behind it, but it does not cover everything. Proper names, technical terms and esoteric words may well be unrecognised and be thrown up as 'errors'.

Word has an additional check-as-you-type facility (see opposite). Even in Word, it is often best to run a spell check after you have finished typing – especially if you have a lot of typing to do and need to watch the keyboard rather than the screen!

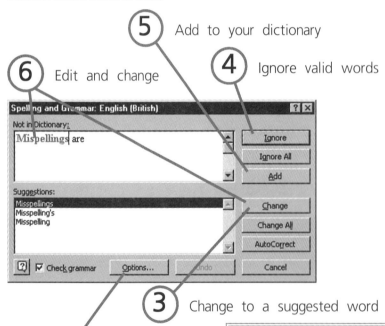

(5) Add to your dictionary

(6) Edit and change

(4) Ignore valid words

(3) Change to a suggested word

Use the Options button to set your preferences (see opposite)

Basic steps

1 If you want to check **part** of a document, or a block of cells in a spreadsheet, select it.

2 Open the **Tools** menu and select **Spelling** or click.

❑ **When a word is not recognised you can:**

3 Select a **Suggestion** and click ⬚ Change ⬚.

or

4 If it is a valid word click ⬚ Ignore ⬚.

or

5 ⬚ Add ⬚ to put it in a custom dictionary.

or

6 Click in the **Not in Dictionary** slot, edit the word then click ⬚ Change ⬚.

Take note

If you haven't already set up a dictionary for your own special words, click the Options button to open the Spelling options panel and use the Custom Dictionaries button.

Basic steps

1 On the **Spelling** dialog box, click **Options**.

2 Turn the settings on or off as desired.

❑ **Fine-tuning grammar**

3 Click ⬚ Se_t_tings... ⬚.

4 Pick a **Writing style**.

5 Turn other checks on or off as desired.

6 Click **OK**.

Use this to find out how readable your text is. If you are writing for an adult audience, aim for a readability of Grade 7 (a reading age of 12) – any lower is patronising; higher is hard work for most people.

Spelling and grammar options

Probably the key options here are whether or not to check spelling and grammar as you type – some people will find that it interrupts their flow, while others prefer to correct errors as they go.

Only use this if you want to have different specialist dictionaries for different types of jobs

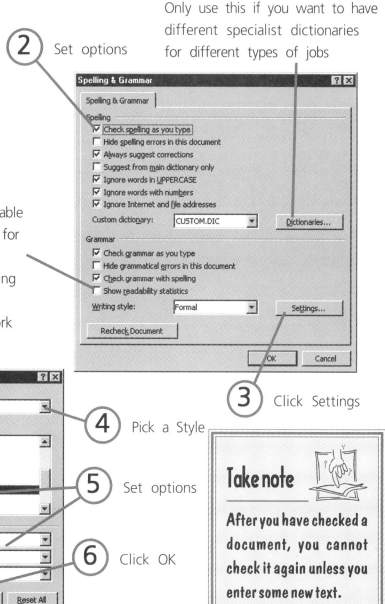

(2) Set options

(3) Click Settings

(4) Pick a Style

(5) Set options

(6) Click OK

Take note

After you have checked a document, you cannot check it again unless you enter some new text.

Summary

- **Text** can be selected with either the mouse or keys, or a combination of both. **Objects** can be selected by clicking on them, or dragging an outline round them with the mouse. The **same selection techniques** apply in all applications.

- **Font** types, sizes and styles can be set from the Formatting toolbar or the Fonts dialog box. The dialog box also has additional control options.

- Text can be **aligned** to the Left or Right margins, Centred between them or Justified up to both.

- **Indents** give a structure to text.

- **Bullets** can be easily added to lists. The default bullets can be replaced by any characters you choose.

- Excel and Word have ready made **styles** that can be applied to text. They can be modified and new ones created.

- The **Autoformat** facility gives you standard formats for common documents and tables of data.

- The **AutoCorrect** routine recognises and corrects mistakes as you type. This may need customising to stop it 'correcting' intentional irregularities.

- If you make mistakes, you can **Undo** them – and if you undo too many actions, you can **Redo** them again!

- The **Spelling checker** has a good dictionary, and you can build your own to hold special terms and names that are not in the main one.

6 Sharing data

Alternative approaches

There are a number of different ways to share data between applications. The first three bring a selected object or block of data into a second application. They use the Edit Copy and Paste commands in various ways.

- **Simple paste** – the text, table, picture or whatever becomes an integral part of the host document, dropping all connection to the application in which it was created. Use this method where the host document's application can handle any editing or reformatting that you might want to do to the pasted-in data.

- **Embedding** – the pasted-in data forms an independent object within the document. It loses its connection to the original data, but can be edited by its own application *within the host document*. Use this method if you want to be able to edit the object using its original application.

- **Linking** – the pasted-in data retains a full connection to the original data and its application. Any changes in the source data are automatically reflected in the copy, and the original file can be edited – by calling up its application – from within the host document. This is the method to use for reports and presentations where you want to ensure that all the data is up to date.

Copy and Paste

The first step in sharing data is to go to the source document, select the object or block of text and copy it, using either the **Edit – Copy** command or . What you do then depends upon whether you want to copy, embed or link the data, and what format you want it in.

- Use  or **Edit – Paste** to copy in the data, using the default format. This will be either Formatted Text or Picture, as applicable.

- Use **Edit – Paste Special** to embed or link, or to select your own format for copied data.

Paste As formats

Word, Excel, PowerPoint (or other) **Object** – use this for embedding;

Formatted Text – the text retains its fonts, styles, etc, but may be edited by the host application;

Unformatted Text – plain text, editable by the host;

Picture and **Bitmap** – scalable graphics; Pictures can give better printed images.

Take note

The range of As formats, and whether or not the data can be linked depends upon the source application and the nature of the data. (See the table on page 100.)

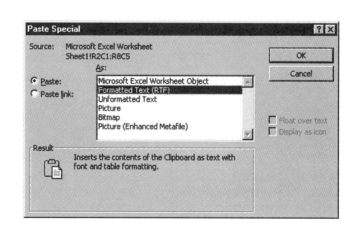

Copying

Using the and ⊟ buttons is the quickest and simplest way to get data from one application into another, but the data is pasted differently in different applications.

① Select the data ② Copy it

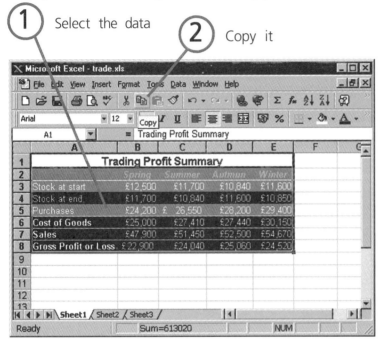

③ Copy to the Clipboard

⑦ Paste into place

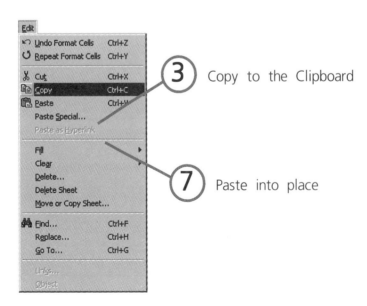

1 In the source application, select the object or block of text or cells to be copied.

2 Click ⊞.

or

3 Pull down the **Edit** menu and select **Copy**.

4 Go to the host document.

5 To paste as *text*, point the cursor to where the data is to be placed.

6 Click 📋.

or

7 Pull down the **Edit** menu and select **Paste**.

Tip

If you do a lot of copy and paste work, learn the keyboard shortcuts:

[Ctrl] –[C] to Copy

[Ctrl] –[V] to Paste

Excel to Word

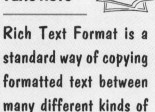
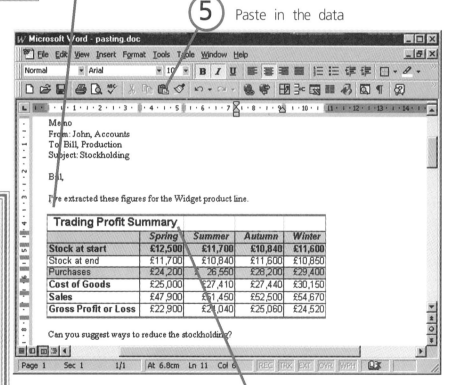 or **Edit – Paste** brings in the data in Rich Text Format, and creates a Word table.

● As it is *text*, it can be edited within Word in the usual fashion;

● As it is *Rich Text*, its font, size, borders, etc. are retained.

④ Position the cursor

⑤ Paste in the data

Memo
From: John, Accounts
To: Bill, Production
Subject: Stockholding

Bill,

I've extracted these figures for the Widget product line.

Trading Profit Summary

	Spring	Summer	Autumn	Winter
Stock at start	£12,500	£11,700	£10,840	£11,600
Stock at end	£11,700	£10,840	£11,600	£10,850
Purchases	£24,200	26,550	£28,200	£29,400
Cost of Goods	£25,000	£27,410	£27,440	£30,150
Sales	£47,900	£51,450	£52,500	£54,670
Gross Profit or Loss	£22,900	£24,040	£25,060	£24,520

Can you suggest ways to reduce the stockholding?

Individual columns and rows, and the contents of any of the cells can be edited and reformatted as needed.

93

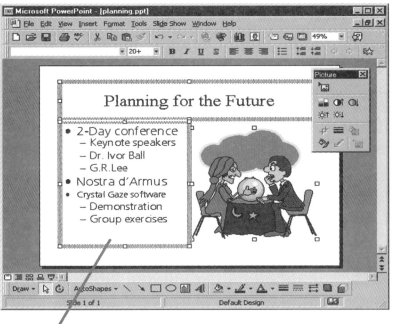

Selected objects can be pasted in as a single picture.
This can be scaled or cropped to size.

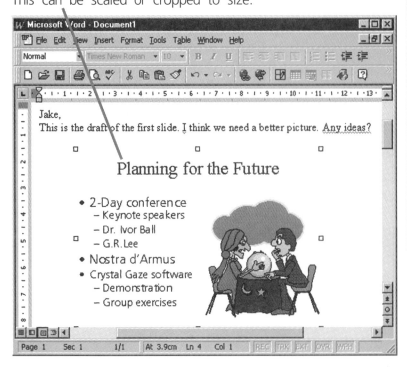

❑ If you select a group of objects from a slide, then Paste them, the objects come in separately, and the text and pictures can then be edited within Word. However, PowerPoint uses BIG font sizes, and the pasted objects are likely to swamp your document.

❑ If the PowerPoint objects are being brought in to illustrate a Word document, use Paste Special, and bring in the group as a Picture for a easier handling.

❑ If you want to take text from PowerPoint into Word, use Paste Special and bring it in as unformatted text – it will be far smaller!

Word to PowerPoint

- ❏ If you 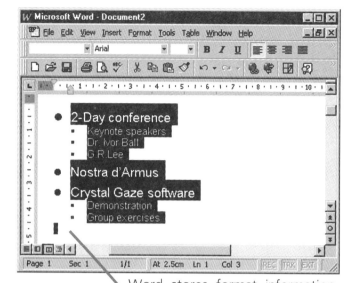 Word text onto a blank area of a slide, it comes in as a Picture.

- ❏ If you Paste into a *Click to add text* area, it is copied in as formatted text, but with all font sizes a few points larger.

- ❏ If you use Insert – Text Box and Paste into there, all text is formatted to the same, larger, font size.

Word stores format information at the end of paragraphs – copy an extra line to make sure all the text is formatted.

A simple Paste brings Word text in as a Picture

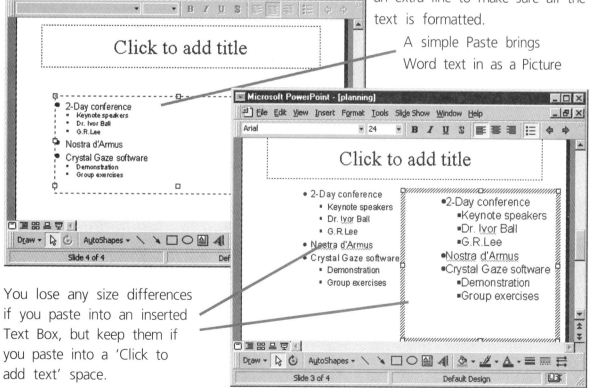

You lose any size differences if you paste into an inserted Text Box, but keep them if you paste into a 'Click to add text' space.

Embedding

Sometimes a simple paste embeds an object – e.g. an Excel table in a PowerPoint slide – but to be certain that an object is embedded, it is best use the Paste Special command.

1 Select the object to be pasted.

2 In the host document, use **Edit – Paste Special..**

3 Set the **As** option to an **Object** of the original application.

4 Select **Paste**.

5 Click **OK**.

④ Select Paste

③ Use the Object format

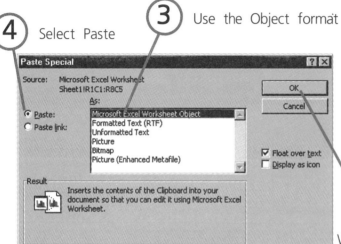

⑤ Click OK

When you edit an embedded object, the tools change to suit the object.

Take note

The embedded object is only a copy of the original data. If you edit an embedded object, it does not affect the data in the original file and vice versa.

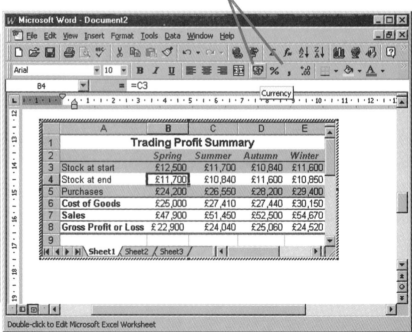

	A	B	C	D	E
1	**Trading Profit Summary**				
2		*Spring*	*Summer*	*Autumn*	*Winter*
3	Stock at start	£12,500	£11,700	£10,840	£11,600
4	Stock at end	£11,700	£10,840	£11,600	£10,850
5	Purchases	£24,200	£26,550	£28,200	£29,400
6	**Cost of Goods**	£25,000	£27,410	£27,440	£30,150
7	**Sales**	£47,900	£51,450	£52,500	£54,670
8	**Gross Profit or Loss**	£22,900	£24,040	£25,060	£24,520
9					

Double-click to Edit Microsoft Excel Worksheet

Basic steps

❏ **Edit within the host**

1 Double click on the object to open a limited version.

or

2 Right click to open the short menu and choose ...**Object – Edit**.

3 Edit and click anywhere off the object to close the application.

❏ **Edit in the application**

4 Right click to open the short menu and choose ...**Object – Open**.

5 Edit, and use **Close and Return...** to exit.

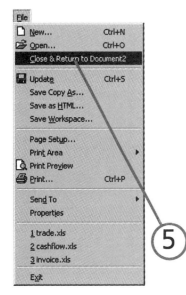

Editing embedded objects

Working with the tools of the host application, the only changes you can make to an embedded object are its size and position. If you want to edit or reformat its content, you must use its original application.

● You can run a limited version, within the host application;

or

● Open the full version of the original application and work on the object there.

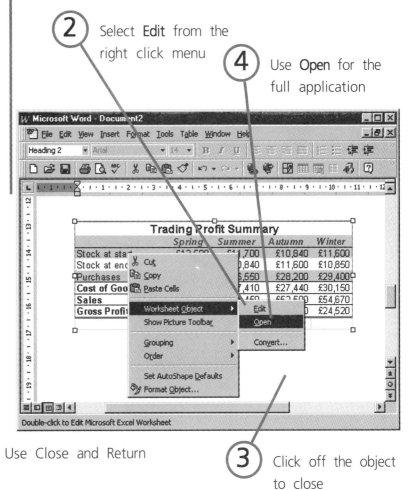

② Select **Edit** from the right click menu

④ Use **Open** for the full application

⑤ Use Close and Return

③ Click off the object to close

97

Linking

The one crucial difference between embedding and linking is that with a linked object, there is only one set of data. When you edit the original file – the source data – the contents of the linked object are changed to match.

1 Copy the block of text or object to be linked.

2 In the host document, open the **Edit** menu and select **Paste Special**.

3 Select **Paste Link**.

4 If you have a choice of **As** formats, select the most suitable one for the job.

5 Click **OK**.

① Copy the source data

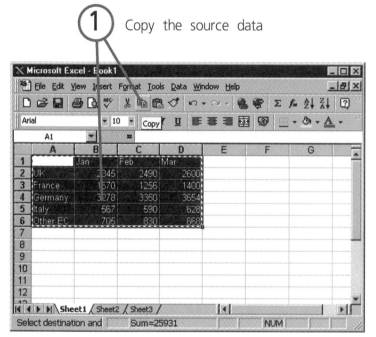

③ Select Paste Link

④ Pick a format

⑤ Click OK

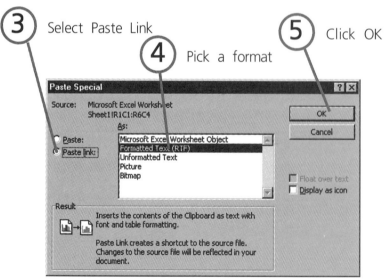

Tip

The type of data that is being linked in determines the choice of As formats (see page 100). When in doubt, use the Object format.

Editing linked objects

All linked objects can be edited by double-clicking on them to call up their original application. Those pasted in the Object format can only be edited this way.

In Object, Picture or Bitmap format, you can alter the size and position of the linked object.

With Formatted or Plain Text, you can also edit them using the host application's tools – though these edits will only last until the link is updated. This is only worth doing if you want to prettify something for immediate printing.

The month names have been edited to appear in full in this linked object. (Compare them with the Excel table opposite.) However, as soon as that Excel file is edited, or when the file is next opened, the link will be updated and the original headings restored.

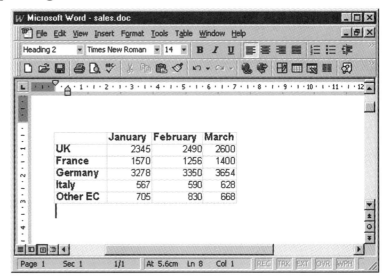

	January	February	March
UK	2345	2490	2600
France	1570	1256	1400
Germany	3278	3350	3654
Italy	567	590	628
Other EC	705	830	668

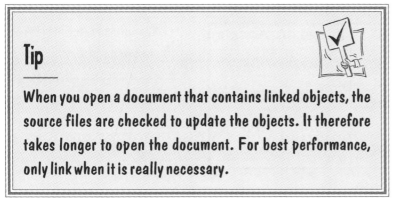

Paste/Paste Link formats

The As formats for Pasting vary with the nature of the data and the source application. They are generally – but not always – what you might expect.

Word

Data type	Paste formats	Paste Link formats
Text	Picture Formatted Text Unformatted Text	Word Object
Table	Picture Formatted Text Unformatted Text	Word Object
Drawing	Picture	*not possible*

Excel

Data type	Paste formats	Paste Link formats
Cell block	Picture Bitmap Formatted Text Unformatted Text	Excel Object *see Take note*
Graph	Picture	Excel Object

PowerPoint

Data type	Paste formats	Paste Link formats
Text	Picture Formatted Text Unformatted Text	*not possible*
ClipArt	Picture MS Drawing Object	*not possible*

Take note

When embedding, you can only ever use the Object format.

A block of cells from Excel can be linked into Word in any of the Paste formats, but only as an Object into PowerPoint.

Tip

You can create Hyperlinks between files – see page 142.

Inserted objects

Complete files can be linked into documents using the **Insert Object** command. Though the whole file is linked, not all of it will be displayed – you will see part of a Word or Excel document, or the first slide of a presentation. If you edit it, you can access the rest, or scroll to a different part of the document to change the visible area.

Inserted file objects can be:

- created at the time, from within the host document, or loaded in from file;

- either embedded or linked;

- displayed normally or present just as icons. In either case, the Edit and Open options for the source application are on the short menu.

Word

The options selected in these menus are what you get if you simply double-click on an inserted object.

PowerPoint

Excel

With a linked object, Edit and Open both call up the full application. If the object is not linked, Edit gives you the limited version of the application, within the host document.

Inserting an object

Once you have decided what you want to insert, and whether to place it as an icon or displayed object, the actual insertion is easy.

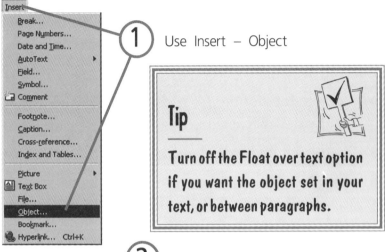

Use Insert – Object

Tip

Turn off the Float over text option if you want the object set in your text, or between paragraphs.

1 Open the **Insert** menu and select **Object**.

2 Switch to the **Create from File** panel (it's an option in PowerPoint).

3 Click **Browse...** to locate the file.

4 Turn on **Link to file**, if wanted, or leave it off to embed the file.

5 If you want the file as a visible object, click **OK**.

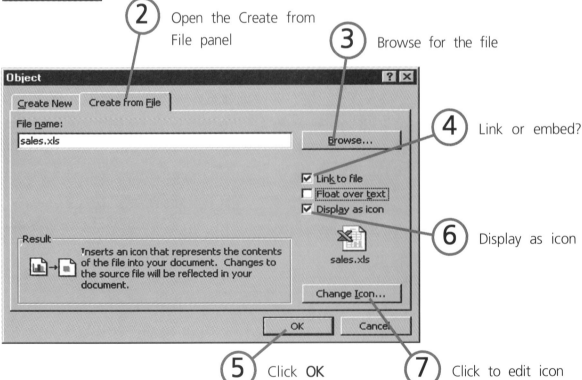

② Open the Create from File panel

③ Browse for the file

④ Link or embed?

⑥ Display as icon

⑤ Click OK

⑦ Click to edit icon

Basic steps

Icons for links

1 Follow steps 1 to 4 opposite.

6 Turn on the **Display as Icon** option.

7 Click [Change Icon...].

8 Check out icons in the list to see if there is one you prefer.

9 Replace the filename with a brief **Caption**.

10 Click **OK**.

If you want your readers to open (or run) the linked file to see it properly, it may be better to place it as an icon. Most computer users nowadays need little prompting to click an icon, though they may well need prompting to click on a spreadsheet table, block of text or other image.

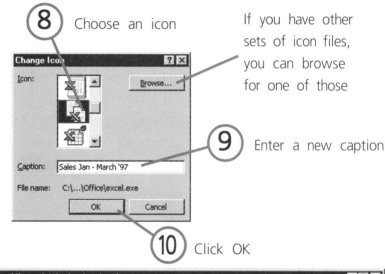

(8) Choose an icon

If you have other sets of icon files, you can browse for one of those

(9) Enter a new caption

(10) Click OK

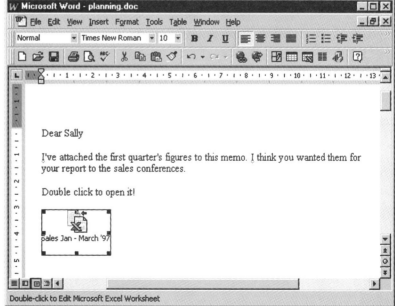

Summary

- The **Edit** – **Copy** and **Paste** commands can be used to copy data from one application to another.
  Depending upon the type of data and the applications, the copy may become an integral part of the target document, or may be embedded in it.

- **Embedded** objects can be edited by calling up their original application from within their new document.

- **Linked** objects retain the connection to their original file. If this is edited, the changes will be seen in the new document.

- Data can be pasted or paste linked into a document, in a **variety of formats**. The choice of formats depends upon the type of data and the source application.

- Files from different applications can be included in documents as **Inserted objects**.

- Linked and Inserted objects can be displayed in their normal format or as **icons**.

7 Binders

Binders and sections

The concept of the Binder is simple but effective. If you have a number of documents – from the same or different Office applications – that are regularly used together, you can store them in one binder file, rather than in separate application files.

Working in the Binder, you can:

- keep related files together, opening and saving all the documents in one operation;

- print all of the documents at once – though selected documents can also be printed individually;

- switch quickly and easily from one application to another;

- copy formats, styles and data between documents more easily.

Sections

The documents in a binder file are referred to as *sections*. Once it has been set up, you would normally leave the composition of a binder alone, but it is not fixed permanently. An existing file can be inserted into a binder as a new section, and sections, created within a binder, can be saved as separate files.

Tip

As with any Office application, you can open a binder document from the File – Open shortcut tool, but it is often easier to work from the Binder shortcut.

File – Open

Binder

The Binder display

The Binder itself is little more than a means of holding and accessing documents. It offers an almost blank display and a limited menu. Once you have opened a binder file, the display will be dominated by the application of the current document within the binder.

The slim panel down the left side is the means of switching between documents. It can be tucked out of the way when not needed, by clicking ⊞ on the far left of the menu bar.

The Section menu has options for adding documents to a new binder

The Section menu is added to every application's menu bar

Click to close and reopen the control panel

Double click to switch to the document

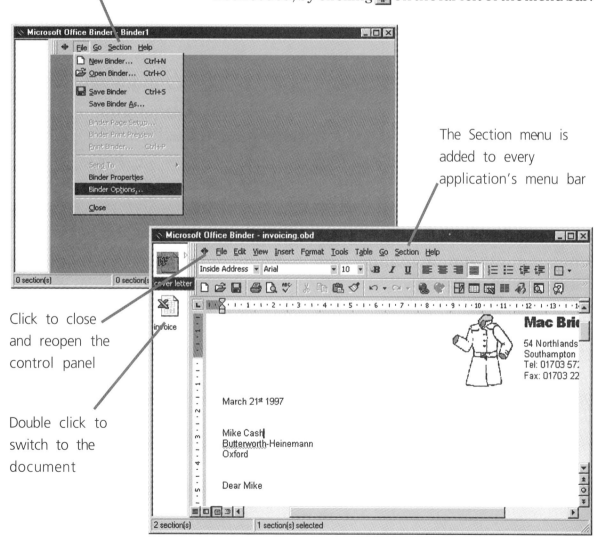

Creating a new binder

You will probably start most of your binders from scratch, though you should have at least one template (Report). You can also create your own templates if you regularly produce sets of documents to the same patterns.

1 Click on the Office Toolbar.

2 Open the **File** menu and select **New**.

❏ **Starting from scratch**

3 Select **Blank Binder**.

❏ **Using a template**

4 Open the **Binders** panel.

5 Pick a template.

6 Click **OK**.

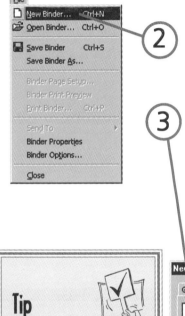

② Use File – New Binder

③ Pick Blank Binder from the General panel

④ Open the Binders panel

⑤ Select a template

Tip

Have a look at the sample Report Binder as it demonstrates some of the key concepts. You may also find that it can be a good basis for your own reports, or can be adapted to suit.

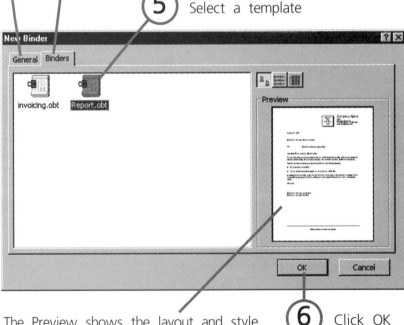

The Preview shows the layout and style of the first document in the binder

⑥ Click OK

108

Basic steps

Adding sections

❑ **To create a document**

1 From the **Section** menu select **Add**.

2 Open a panel and select a template.

or

3 Open the **General** panel and select an application.

❑ **To add from file**

4 From the **Section** menu select **Add from File**.

5 At the **Add from File** dialog box, pick a file.

6 Click [Add].

The documents that are bound into it can be created from new – within the binder – or pulled in from existing files.

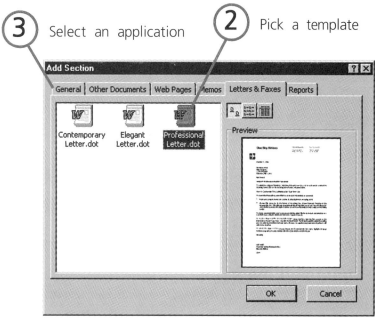

③ Select an application   ② Pick a template

① Add a new document

④ or Add from File   ⑤ Pick a file   ⑥ Click Add

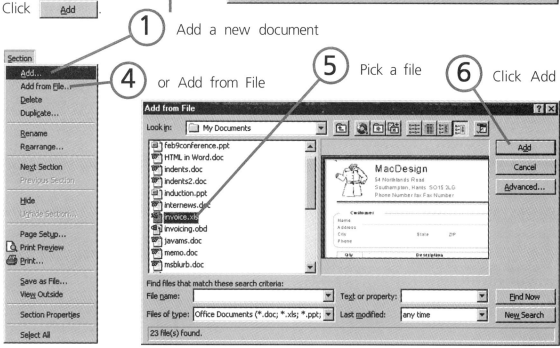

109

Sections and files

If you have a number of files that you want to pull into a binder, it may be quicker to drag them in from their Explorer folder.

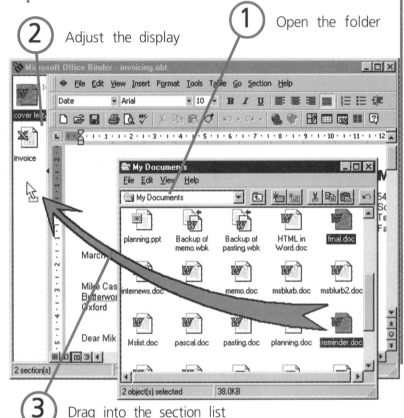

❑ **Dragging files**

1 Run **Explorer** or **My Computer** and open the file's folder.

2 Adjust the display so that the Binder section pane is in view.

3 Drag the file into the Binder, dropping it into place in the list.

❑ **Saving sections**

4 Switch to the section.

5 From the **Section** menu select **Save as File**.

6 Complete the **Save** dialog box as normal.

Saving sections

Whether the sections were created within the binder, or brought in from file, once in place they form into a single structure – a binder document is saved as one file. However, it is possible to save a section as a separate file if required.

Basic steps

1 Switch to the source document.
2 From the **Section** menu, select **Duplicate**.
3 Choose where the new document is to fit.
4 Click **OK**.
5 Click in the duplicate's name and edit it

Duplicating sections

One of the useful features of binders is that you can easily duplicate a section. For instance, if you wanted several Word documents, all with the same letterhead, you could design the first, then duplicate that document to give you a basis for the others.

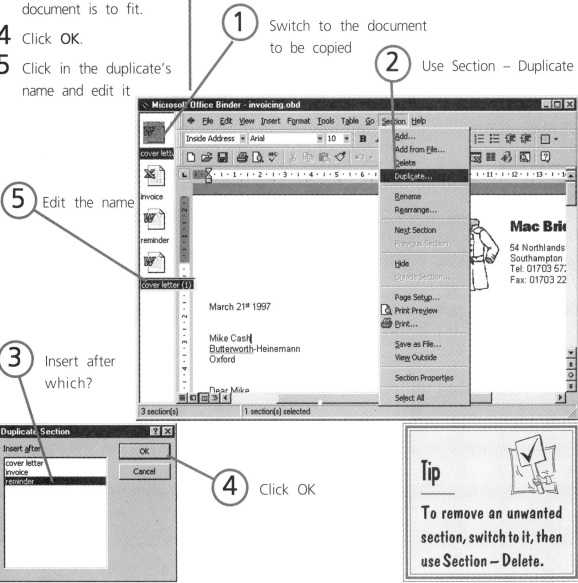

1 Switch to the document to be copied

2 Use Section – Duplicate

5 Edit the name

3 Insert after which?

4 Click OK

Tip

To remove an unwanted section, switch to it, then use Section – Delete.

Multiple views

An apparent drawback to the binder is that it can only display one section at a time. There is a simple way round this. The View Outside facility lets you open a free-standing copy of the application to handle a section.

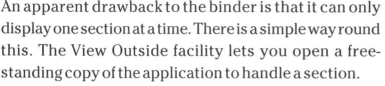

Use Section – View Outside

① Select a section

④ Adjust the display

⑤ Close and return

③ Open the other section

Basic steps

1 Switch to the section you want to view.

2 From the **Section** menu select **View Outside**.

3 Back in the Binder, open the other section you want to view.

4 Set the display so that you can flip between binder and application.

5 Use **File – Close and return** to exit from the outside application.

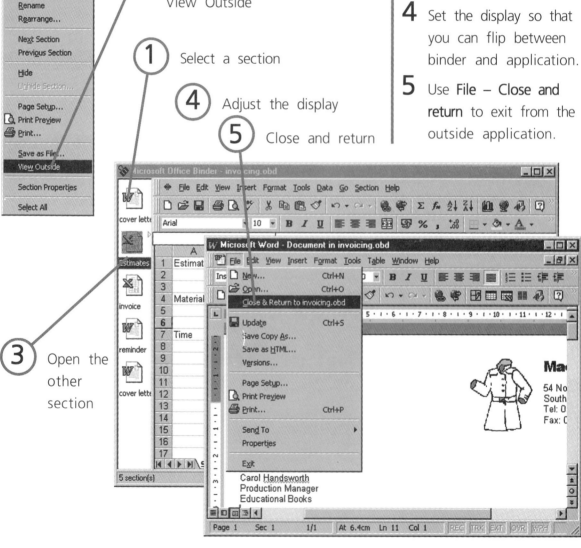

Basic steps

1 Open the first section to be printed.

2 Hold **[Ctrl]** and click the other sections.

3 Open the **File** menu and select **Print Binder**.

4 Set the **Print What** option to **All** or **Selected** sections.

5 Set the **Numbering** to **Continuous** or **Restart** each section.

6 Click **OK**.

You can print all the sections of the binder at once or select one or more for printing. If you are printing a selection, this must be set up first.

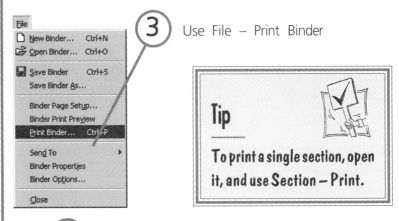

③ Use File – Print Binder

> **Tip**
>
> To print a single section, open it, and use Section – Print.

④ Print All or a Selection

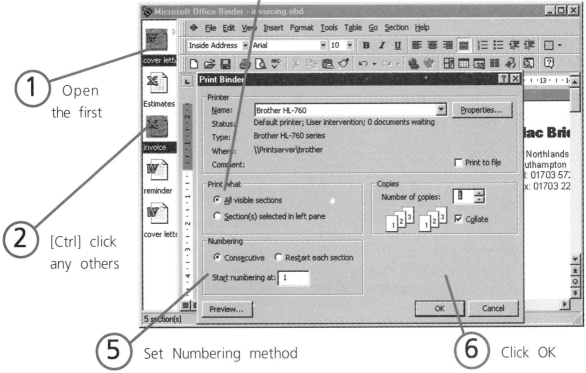

① Open the first

② [Ctrl] click any others

⑤ Set Numbering method

⑥ Click OK

Summary

❑ A **Binder** holds a set of documents from the same or different applications.

❑ The documents in binders are referred to as **sections.**

❑ An **empty Binder window** is little more than a frame with a small section of commands for opening binders and adding sections.

❑ An **application window**, within a binder, has a Section menu and panel on the left side holding section icons.

❑ There is a **sample binder** (report.obt) that you can experiment with, or use as a base for your own.

❑ **New binders** are created by pulling in existing files or creating new documents from within the binder.

❑ Sections can be **saved as separate files** if needed.

❑ If you need to see more than one section at a time, the **View Outside** feature lets you open a separate copy of an application to edit a section.

❑ You can **print** the whole binder or one or more selected sections in one operation.

8 Working with Graphics

Importing pictures

'A picture is worth a thousand words.' That philosophy can be applied to many types of documents.

- Your logo on letterheads and invoices will make your company instantly identifiable;

- Pictures of your products in your catalogues should sell them better than any description;

- Diagrams are often essential for communicating technical information and other complex concepts.

❏ **Pictures in Word**

1 Open the **Insert** menu, point to **Picture** then select **From File...**

2 Switch to the picture's folder.

3 If there are lots of files, use the **File type** slot to filter out the right type.

4 Pick a picture, checking its preview.

5 Click [Insert].

Tip

JPG, GIF, Photo CD and other standard graphics files can be imported if you install the graphic converters for them.

① Use Insert – Picture – From FIle

② Go to the folder

④ Pick a picture

⑤ Click Insert

③ Set the File type

If the picture may be changed, tick Link to file to have it updated automatically

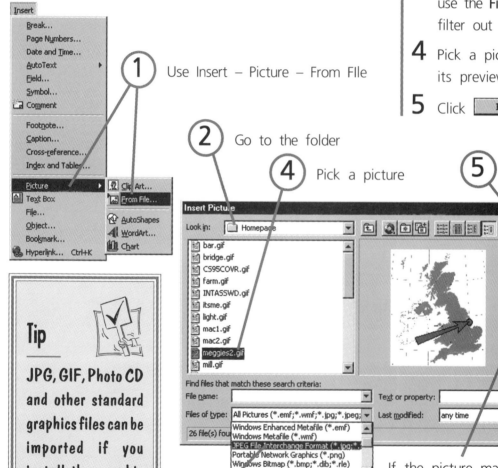

Basic steps

1 Use **Insert** — **Picture** – **Clip Art**.

or

2 Open the **Insert** menu and select **Object**.

3 At the **Insert Object** dialog box, select **Clip Gallery**.

4 Open the Clip Art panel.

5 Choose a **Category**.

6 Scroll through and select a picture.

7 Click [**Insert**].

Clip Art

Clip Art pictures from the Clip Gallery can be inserted into any application – but don't overdo it. There's so much clip art around that you must use it selectively to have any impact.

③ Select Clip Gallery

These are video clips

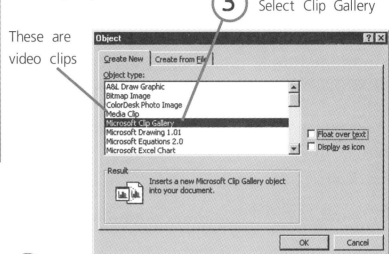

④ Go to Clip Art

⑤ Choose a Category

⑥ Pick a picture

⑦ Click Insert

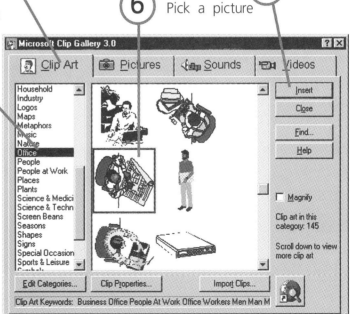

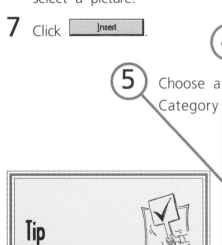

Tip

People have to be determined to read solid text, but will glance at illustrated material – and once you've got their interest, they might read on.

Formatting pictures

The final appearance of any picture – Clip Art, file or Drawing (see page 120) – can be adjusted at any point. Use the mouse to change the size, shape or position, or open the Format picture menu to add a border, fine-tune the brightness and contrast, or set how text wraps around it.

Basic steps

1 Select the picture.

2 Drag on a handle to adjust the size or shape.

3 Drag anywhere within the area to move.

4 Right click for the short menu and select **Format Picture**.

5 Work through the panels as required.

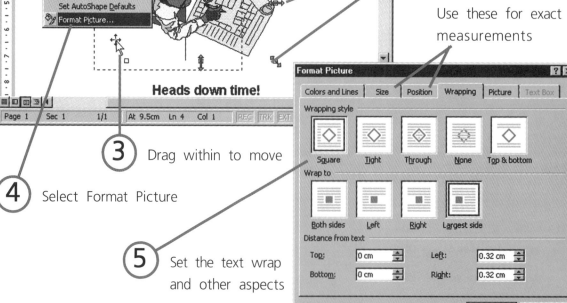

① Select the picture

② Drag a handle to resize

Use these for exact measurements

③ Drag within to move

④ Select Format Picture

⑤ Set the text wrap and other aspects

Sound and video clips

1 Use **Insert – Object** and select the **Clip Gallery**.

2 Switch to **Video** or **Sounds**.

3 Select a clip.

4 Click **Play** to test.

5 Click **Insert**.

You can stop playing video clips, but sounds keep on until they reach their end – and some sound clips are far too long!

Sound and video clips are particularly useful in PowerPoint presentations, but can be added to other documents if required.

② Open Sounds or Video

③ Select a clip

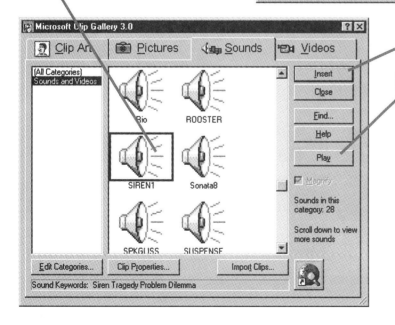

⑤ Click Insert

④ Click Play

Tip

If you have an Internet connection, you can get more clips from the Web – just click the shortcut (see page 133).

Drawing pictures

If you want to create new diagrams or images, pick out points on imported pictures, or simply add arrows, blobs or blocks of background colour, there is a handy set of tools on the Drawing toolbar.

In a drawn picture, each item remains separate and can be moved, resized, recoloured or deleted at any later time. (Though items can be joined into Groups or placed inside picture frames, for convenient handling.) This is quite different from Paint and similar packages, where each addition becomes merged permanently into the whole picture.

Autoshapes offer a quick way to get neat effects

The Draw menu lets you manipulate elements, singly or in groups.

Basic steps

1 Click ⬛ to open the **Drawing** toolbar.

2 Select an object tool and point and drag to create the item.

3 Adjust the fill and line colour and style.

4 To adjust an existing item, click the Selector tool and click on the item. It can then be moved, deleted, resized or recoloured.

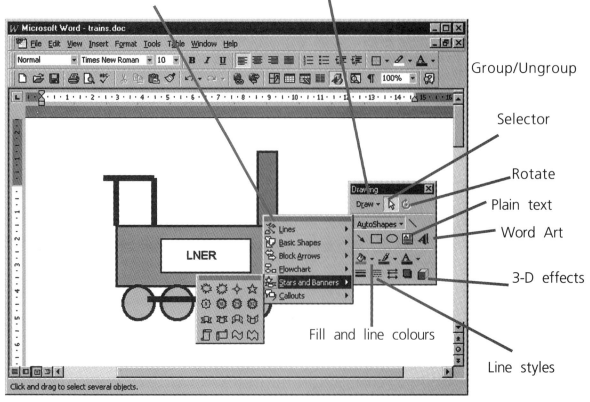

Group/Ungroup

Selector

Rotate

Plain text

Word Art

3-D effects

Fill and line colours

Line styles

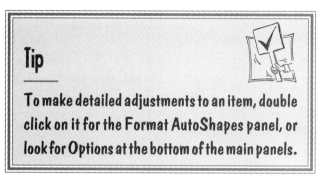

Tip

To make detailed adjustments to an item, double click on it for the Format AutoShapes panel, or look for Options at the bottom of the main panels.

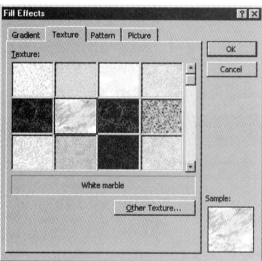

Fill Effects include Gradients and Textures — both good for the backgrounds of boxes. The same Patterns are available here as for Lines.

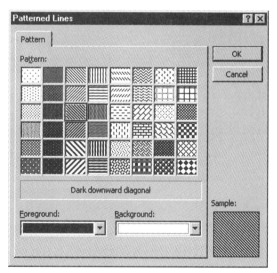

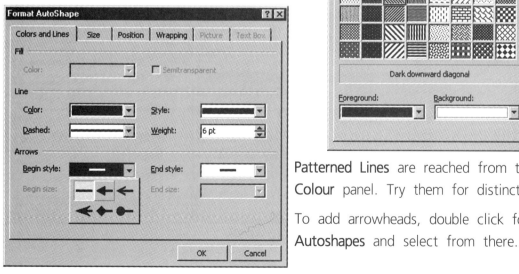

Patterned Lines are reached from the Line Colour panel. Try them for distinctive frames.

To add arrowheads, double click for Format Autoshapes and select from there.

Data maps

One of the clever little extras included in the Office 95 package is the Data Map software – actually, not that little as it occupies over 6 Mb. This can take a table of geographical names and associated values – a Sales by Country summary, for example – and use it to create a map, with the relevant places shaded to show their relative importance. And it does it all by itself!

Basic steps

❏ **Maps in Excel**

1 Set up the data with names and values in adjacent, headed columns.

2 Select the data range.

3 Open the **Insert** menu and select **Map...**

4 Drag an outline where the map is to go.

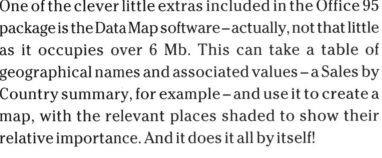

③ Choose Insert – Map...

② Select the data

④ Drag an outline

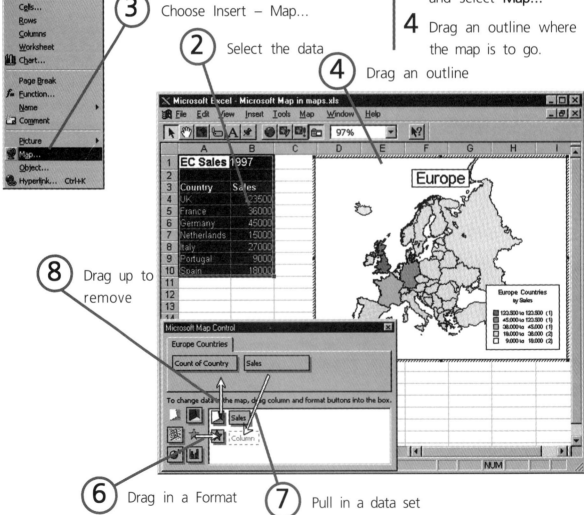

⑧ Drag up to remove

⑥ Drag in a Format

⑦ Pull in a data set

Potential problems

5 Wait – this could take a couple of minutes

❑ **Value indicators**

If you have several sets of values or do not want to use shading...

6 Drag a **Format** button onto the **Format** label.

7 Drag a data set name onto the **Column** label.

8 Remove an unwanted style by dragging the Format button up out of the box.

Format styles

🔲 Shading

🔲 Block Colour

🔲 Dot density

🔲 Graduated symbol

🔲 Pie Chart

🔲 Bar Chart

● The Data Map does have has its limitations. It can handle the world, North and South America, US states, Europe and the UK, but not much else. You may see this panel:

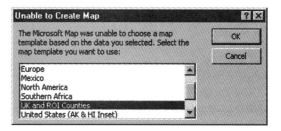

If you do select a map now, it will only be decorative, as the software will not be able to relate your names to any actual places.

● You may be given a choice of map. It doesn't matter if one covers too wide an area. You can set the display to zoom in on the relevant part.

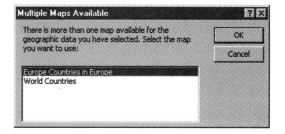

● If the software cannot recognise a name, is will ask you for an alternative. For instance, it doesn't know about 'Holland' but will accept 'Netherlands'.

Annotating the map

There are three types of annotations available.

The Label tool will get the names and values from your data table.

The Pin tool will stick labelled pins in the map.

The Text tool can be used for any other text.

Basic steps

❑ Labels

1 Click ⬜.

2 At the **Map Labels** dialog box, select **Names** or **Values**.

3 With **Values**, if there are several sets, select the column.

4 Point at the area to be labelled and click. Repeat as needed.

5 Click elsewhere on the sheet to end.

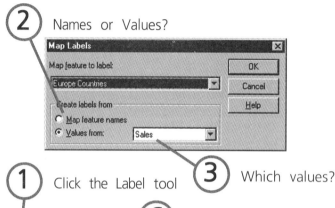

② Names or Values?

① Click the Label tool

③ Which values?

Selector

⑥ Click the Pin tool

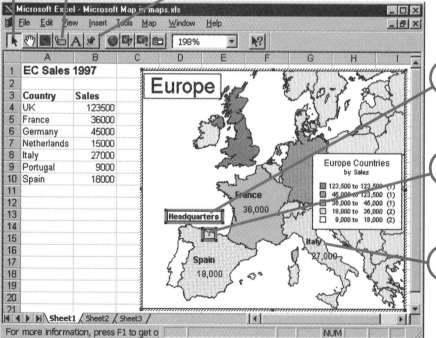

⑨ Drag into place

⑧ Click to locate

④ Click to locate

124

❑ Pins

6 Click .

7 At the **Custom Pin Map** dialog box, give a name for the file that will be created.

8 Click to place a pin, then type its label.

9 Switch to the Selector tool and drag the pin to move both, or the label to move it alone.

Basic steps

1 In Word or PowerPoint use **Insert – Object** and select **Microsoft Map.**

2 When the map appears select **Insert – External Data.**

3 Open the Access or Excel file, and select the data table.

4 Continue as for an Excel Data Map.

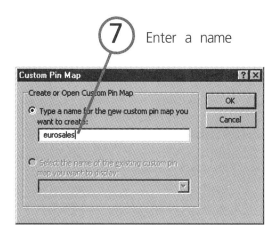

⑦ Enter a name

Maps in Word and PowerPoint

A Data Map can give impact to a report or presentation. Adding one is much the same as in Excel, with one key exception. When you insert a Map Object, you will get a standard (World) map. You must then link to an Access or Excel table to get the data.

① Insert a Map

② Get the data

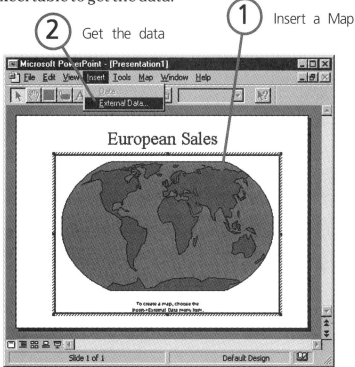

WordArt

If you want a fancy front cover for a report, or a high impact slide, you might like to investigate WordArt. The Office 97 version is significantly better and easier to use than the previous WordArt. With it, you can shape and style text in ways that go far beyond the standard Font Formatting tools.

1 Open the **Insert** menu and select **Picture** then **WordArt**.

2 Select a style from the **Gallery**.

3 Click **OK**.

4 Enter your text at the prompt.

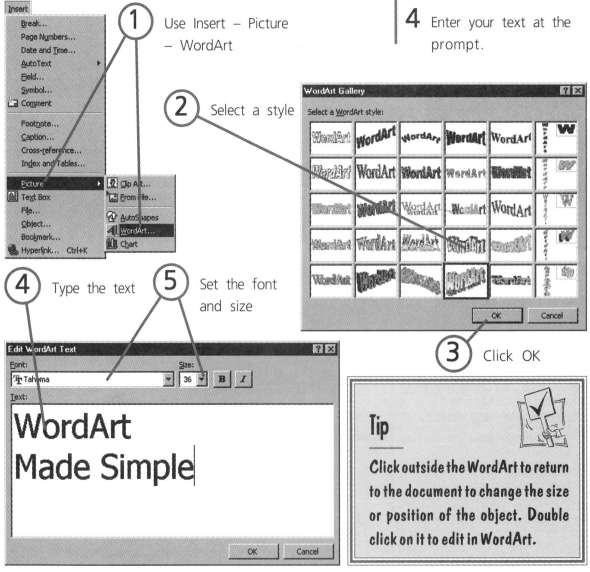

Use Insert – Picture – WordArt

Select a style

Type the text

Set the font and size

Click OK

Tip

Click outside the WordArt to return to the document to change the size or position of the object. Double click on it to edit in WordArt.

5 Set the font and size.

6 Use the tools to adjust the shape, colour and other effects.

7 Click outside the WordArt area to end.

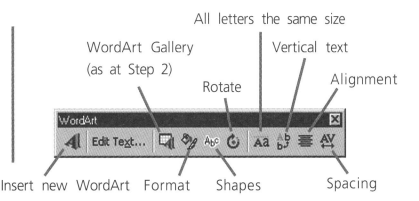

All letters the same size

WordArt Gallery (as at Step 2)

Vertical text

Rotate

Alignment

Insert new WordArt   Format   Shapes   Spacing

6 Set other effects

The **Shapes** fix the outline of the text

Alignment options set the lines of text within the overall shape

Spacing options are mainly used where there are several lines of text

Quick graphs

If you want to knock up a quick graph in a Word or PowerPoint document, the Graph 97 software will do the job. It gives you a datasheet and related graph, set up with dummy data. All you have to do is replace that data with your own. If you care to spend the time, you can also change the chart style, colours and other aspects of its appearance.

① Select Graph 97

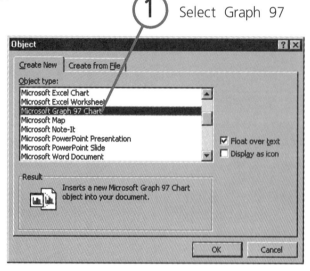

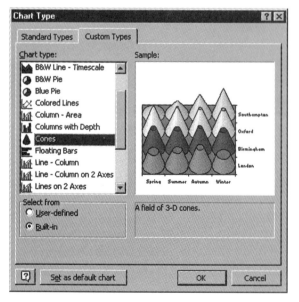

1 Open the **Insert** menu, select **Object** then **Graph 97**.

2 Type your data into the datasheet, adding more columns or rows if needed.

3 Use the tools to change the display – most toggle features on and off.

4 Select an item from the chart and right click for its formatting options.

or

5 Select the element from the drop down list and click the **Formatting** button.

6 Click back into the document and adjust the graph's size.

Tip

There is a full range of normal chart types on the Standard panel – and some striking ones on the Custom panel.

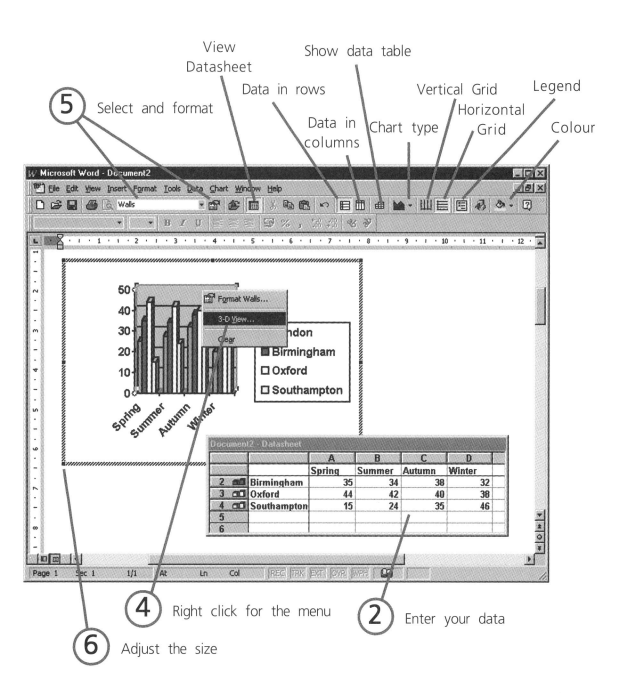

View
Datasheet

Show data table

Data in rows

Select and format

Vertical Grid

Legend

Data in columns

Chart type

Horizontal
Grid

Colour

Right click for the menu

Enter your data

Adjust the size

Summary

❑ You can import **clip art**, **pictures** and other images in most common graphics formats into any Office application, to illustrate or enhance a document.

❑ You can fine-tune the final appearance of any inserted picture through the **Formatting** options.

❑ There is a huge and varied set of **Clip Art** pictures in the **Clip Gallery**.

❑ **Video** and **Sound** clips can be inserted into any documents – though they are probably best reserved for PowerPoint presentations.

❑ The **Drawing** tools can be used to creat diagrams or add lines, arrows or other simple graphics.

❑ The **Data Map** will convert a table of geographic names and related data into a map, with shading to show the relative values.

❑ **WordArt** can be used for headings, splashes and background text. It gives you far more scope for manipulating text than the normal Formatting tools.

❑ To produce a graph from a small table of data quickly, insert a **Graph 97** object.

9 Beyond the desktop

Internet links

In the Microsoft vision of the future, the world is your desktop. They see a time when the Internet will be as accessible as your local area network, and you will exchange ideas and documents as easily with colleagues around the world as you do now with those in your office.

At the time of writing, the next version of Explorer is expected to be released shortly – not *Windows* Explorer, or *Internet* Explorer, just *Explorer*. The same software is used to access the files on your hard disks, the other computers on your local network, the pages of the World Wide Web and everything else that is on-line.

Office 97 takes a big step along that same road, with Web browsing and e-mail facilities in all its applications, and links to Internet resources at key points (see opposite).

The Web toolbar will be familiar to anyone who has used Internet Explorer.

Tip

If you have Internet Explorer or any other Web browser on your system, this will be activated when you try to go anywhere using the Web toolbar in an Office application. You can stop this by going to Windows Explorer and removing or redefining the HTM, HTML and URL File Types. I wouldn't bother. The browser will load up in a few seconds, and it will do a better job.

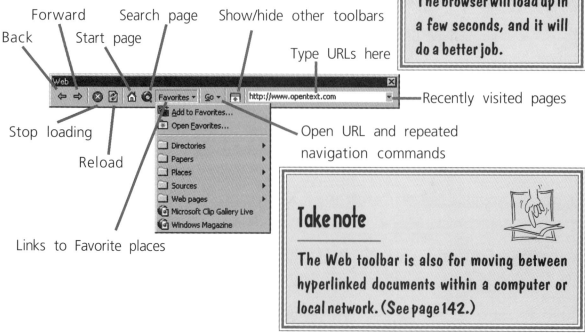

Forward   Search page   Show/hide other toolbars
Back   Start page

Type URLs here

Recently visited pages

Stop loading

Reload

Open URL and repeated navigation commands

Links to Favorite places

Take note

The Web toolbar is also for moving between hyperlinked documents within a computer or local network. (See page 142.)

The Clip Gallery offers a good example of the 'world-is-your-desktop' approach – and of its limitations.

A quick click on 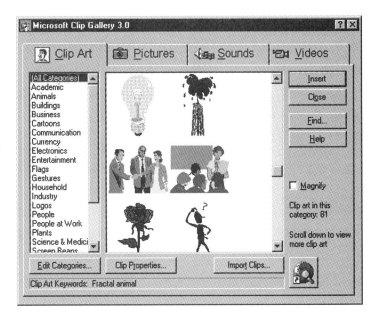 should take you to Microsoft's Clip Gallery on the Web. If you have a fast ISDN connection to the Internet, you will get there quickly. If the Microsoft site, and the main Internet connections, are not too busy, you will be able to find and download files quickly...

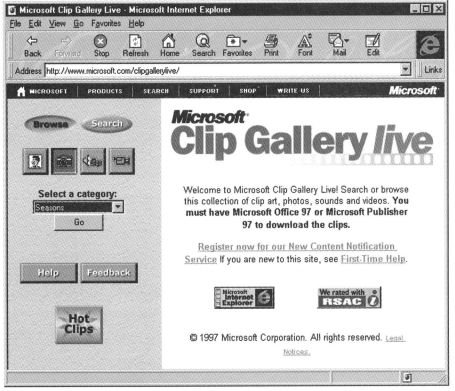

...but if you have a dial-up connection, and the site or the Internet's lines are busy, you will wait ages for your files. It will take a lot more development of the world's telephone connections, and of the Internet's hardware before we will all be able to treat the Internet as a simple extension of our desktops.

Outlook Inbox

The Inbox is the central part of Outlook's mail system, and can be reached from both the Outlook and the Mail sections. The Mail section also has the **Outbox**, where messages sit while awaiting delivery, and **Sent Items**, which is used for storing copies of your outgoing mail.

You must have Microsoft Exchange installed and configured, to be able to use the Inbox – the Inbox is little more than a front-end to Exchange. However, if you use Outlook as your desktop personal organiser, it makes sense to use the Inbox, rather than starting up Exchange.

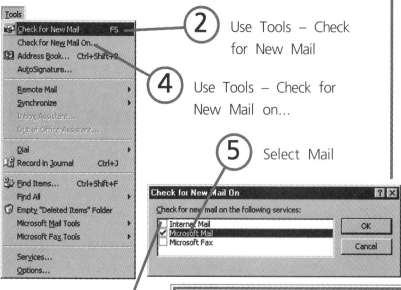

(2) Use Tools – Check for New Mail

(4) Use Tools – Check for New Mail on...

(5) Select Mail

You could also just check your Internet Mail

☐ **Getting all your mail**

1 Turn on your modem, if you want your Internet mail.

2 Open the **Tools** menu and select **Check for New Mail**.

3 Wait, then respond as normal to connect to the Internet.

☐ **Getting mail off a LAN**

4 Open the **Tools** menu and select **Check for New Mail on...**

5 At the dialog box, select **Microsoft Mail** (and **Fax**, if relevant).

Take note

To use Outlook's mail, you must be on a local area network or the Internet (or both), and have Microsoft Exchange in your system. For more information on setting up network or Internet mail, see *Microsoft Networking Made Simple* and *The Internet Made Simple*.

Basic steps

❏ **Reading and replying**

1 Double click on a message, or right-click and select **Open**.

2 Read the message.

3 Use the buttons or the **Compose** menu, and select **Reply** to send to the author, or **Reply to All** to send to all who received a copy, or **Forward** to send a copy to another person.

4 Continue as for sending mail (next page).

① Double-click or select Open

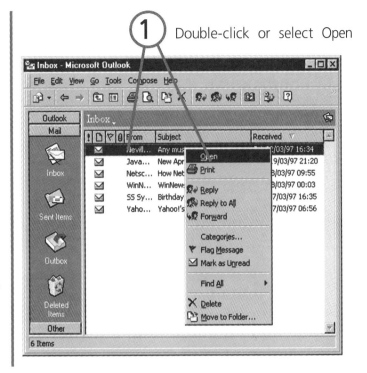

② Read the message

③ Select a Compose option or click a button

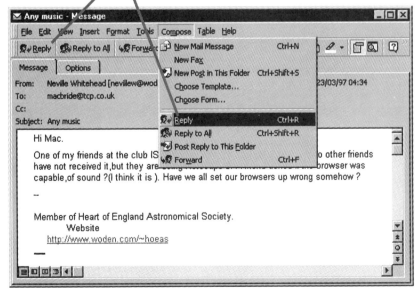

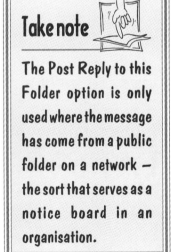

Take note

The Post Reply to this Folder option is only used where the message has come from a public folder on a network — the sort that serves as a notice board in an organisation.

Sending e-mail

E-mail is transforming business (and personal) communications. It is cheap, fast and reliable – and if a message does not get through, your Post server will let you know. But it does need to be used with a bit of thought.

- Type a clear Subject line, so your recipients know that your message is not junk e-mail to be ignored;

- Keep messages short – people have to pay for phone time to download them.

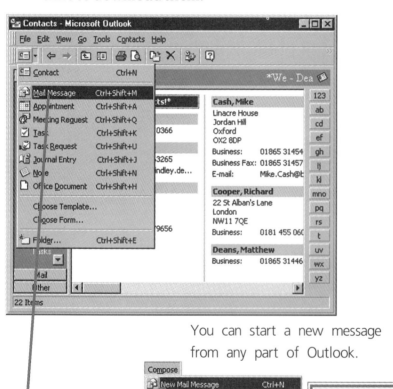

You can start a new message from any part of Outlook.

① Use New Mail Message

Basic steps

1 Open the **New...** menu or **Compose** in the Inbox, and select **New Mail Message**.

2 At the **Compose** window, click `To...`.

3 Drop down the **Show Names** list and select an address book.

4 Select the recipient and click `To ->` or `Cc ->` for copies – repeat if needed.

5 Click **OK**.

6 Type a **Subject**, then your message.

7 Switch to the **Options** panel.

8 Set the **Sensitivity, Delivery** time and other options as required.

9 Click **Send**.

Take note

If an address is not in your Contacts or other address book, you must add it at step 3.

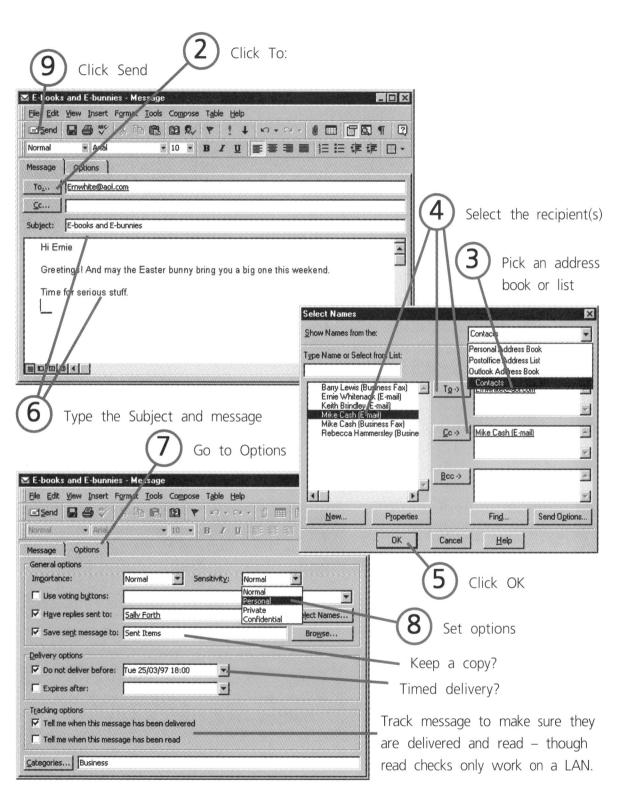

⑨ Click Send

② Click To:

④ Select the recipient(s)

③ Pick an address book or list

⑥ Type the Subject and message

⑦ Go to Options

⑤ Click OK

⑧ Set options

Keep a copy?

Timed delivery?

Track message to make sure they are delivered and read – though read checks only work on a LAN.

Files by wire

For 10 years or more, the experts have been telling us that computers will create the paperless office, but in most offices so far they seem to have created even more paper. Start to reverse that trend with Office 97!

- E-mail documents, from within an application;

- Attach document files to e-mail messages as you compose them;

- Circulate documents, for comments or amendments, by adding a Routing slip;

- Send faxes directly from your computer, without printing first.

❑ **E-mailing documents**

1 From the **File** menu, select **Send** then **Mail Recipient...**

❑ The **Compose** window opens, with the document embedded in the message area.

2 Click ▢To... and select the recipient(s).

3 If the document has been given a Title, it will be copied into the **Subject** line – if not, type a header here.

4 Add a message and send as usual.

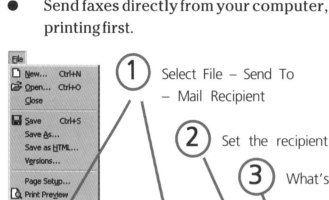

① Select File – Send To – Mail Recipient

② Set the recipient

③ What's it about?

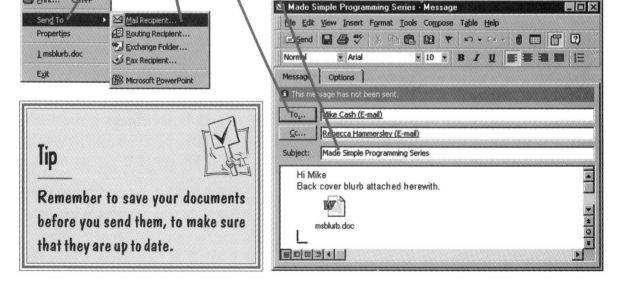

Tip

Remember to save your documents before you send them, to make sure that they are up to date.

Basic steps

Routing slips

1 From the **File** menu, select **Send** then **Routing Recipient…**

2 Click [**Address…**] and select the recipients.

3 Click [**Route**] to circulate the document immediately.

or

4 Click [**Add Slip**] to leave it set for later routing.

If you want several people to see and make comments on a draft document, you can circulate round the internal network, or through your Internet connections, by adding a Routing slip. You can control the order in which the document is circulated, and also what can be done to it.

● Use **Tracked changes** to turn on revision marking, so that you can see what changes have been made;

● Use **Comments**, to allow others to add notes, but not change the document;

● The **Forms** option is only for circulating forms for collecting information.

Tip

To Learn more about using Word, see *Word 97 Made Simple.*

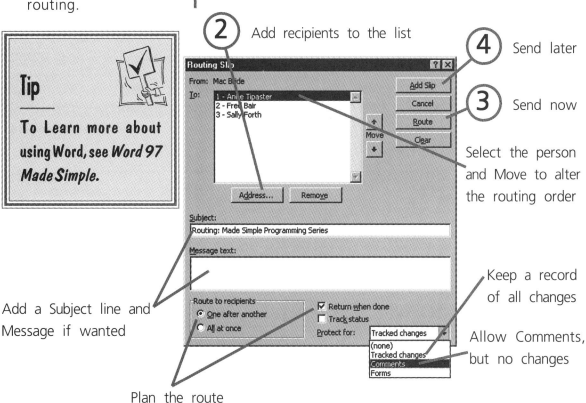

② Add recipients to the list

④ Send later

③ Send now

Select the person and Move to alter the routing order

Add a Subject line and Message if wanted

Keep a record of all changes

Allow Comments, but no changes

Plan the route

139

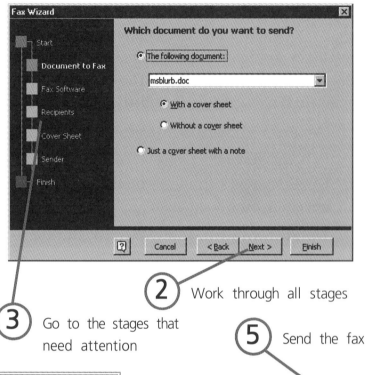

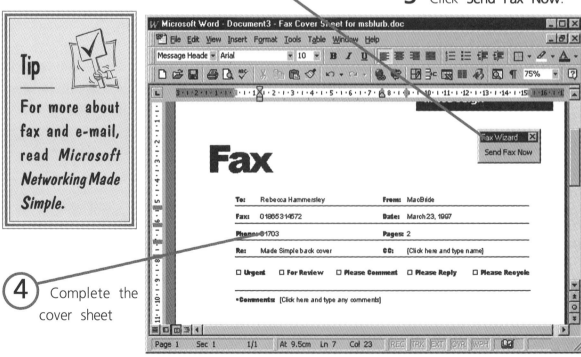

❑ **Sending faxes**

1 From the **File** menu, select **Send** then **Fax Recipient...** to start the **Fax Wizard**.

2 The first time, work through the stages, clicking **Next**.

or

3 On later uses, skip to those stages that need new settings.

4 If there is a **Cover page**, fill in your details.

5 Click **Send Fax Now**.

② Work through all stages

③ Go to the stages that need attention

⑤ Send the fax

④ Complete the cover sheet

Tip

For more about fax and e-mail, read *Microsoft Networking Made Simple*.

Basic steps

Attached files

Any files – from any application, not just Office 97 – can be attached or linked to an e-mail. Use a Link if the recipient is on your local network, and the document file is in a public folder – it is more efficient that actually sending the file.

❑ Attaching files

1 Compose a **New Mail Message** (page 136).

2 Open the **Insert** menu, select **File**.

3 Type the **Filename** or browse for the file.

4 Select the **Link to file** option if appropriate.

5 Send as usual.

① Compose a message

⑤ Send

③ Select the file

② Use Insert – File

④ Just send a Link?

Hyperlinks

A hyperlink can take you from one file to another on the same computer or on a totally different system on the other side of the world. All Office 97 applications can handle hyperlinks. You can create them and travel along them in e-mail messages, Word reports, spreadsheets or databases.

If your document is going to be read by other Office 97 users, and you want to draw their attention to a file on a public folder in your computer or network, or on the Internet, don't embed it or attach it – use a hyperlink.

Basic steps

❑ **Creating a hyperlink**

1 Select the word or phrase (or picture).

2 Use **Insert – Hyperlink** or click 🖳.

3 Type the Internet address or browse for the file to be linked.

4 Click **OK**.

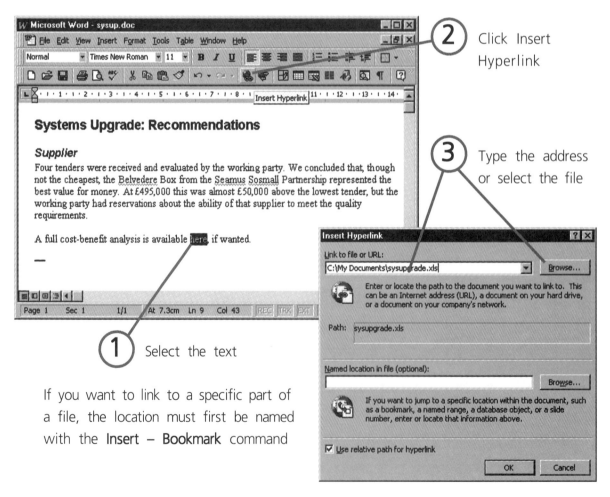

② Click Insert Hyperlink

③ Type the address or select the file

① Select the text

If you want to link to a specific part of a file, the location must first be named with the **Insert – Bookmark** command

Basic steps

❏ **Using hyperlinks**

1 Click on the underlined word or phrase.

2 Wait for the linked document (and its application) to load.

3 The **Web toolbar** will have appeared. Use its **Back** and **Forwards** buttons to navigate between the linked documents.

If you pause the cursor over a link, the hand pointer appears and the address of the file or Web page is shown

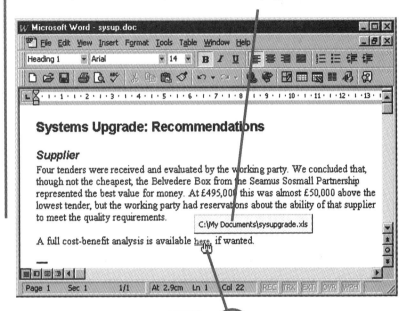

Systems Upgrade: Recommendations

Supplier

Four tenders were received and evaluated by the working party. We concluded that, though not the cheapest, the Belvedere Box from the Seamus Sosmall Partnership represented the best value for money. At £495,000 this was almost £50,000 above the lowest tender, but the working party had reservations about the ability of that supplier to meet the quality requirements.

C:\My Documents\sysupgrade.xls

A full cost-benefit analysis is available here, if wanted.

③ Move between the linked files

① Click on the link

② Wait while it loads

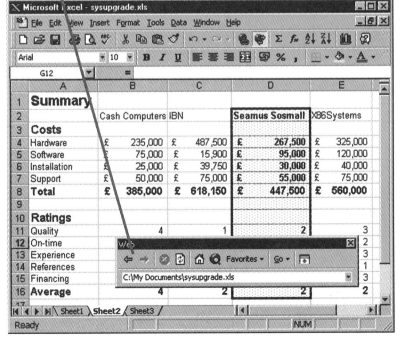

	A	B	C	D	E
1	**Summary**				
2		Cash Computers	IBN	Seamus Sosmall	X86Systems
3	**Costs**				
4	Hardware	£ 235,000	£ 487,500	£ 267,500	£ 325,000
5	Software	£ 75,000	£ 15,900	£ 95,000	£ 120,000
6	Installation	£ 25,000	£ 39,750	£ 30,000	£ 40,000
7	Support	£ 50,000	£ 75,000	£ 55,000	£ 75,000
8	**Total**	£ 385,000	£ 618,150	£ 447,500	£ 560,000
9					
10	**Ratings**				
11	Quality	4	1	2	3
12	On-time				2
13	Experience				3
14	References				1
15	Financing				3
16	**Average**	4	2	2	2

C:\My Documents\sysupgrade.xls

Tip

If you want to create Web pages, use Word's HTML formatting and save the files as HTML. *Word 97 Made Simple* has more on this.

143

Summary

- ❑ **Easy access to the Internet** has been built into all the Office 97 applications.

- ❑ **Finding** and **downloading files** from the Internet can take longer than you think!

- ❑ Use the **Inbox** to fetch and reply to your e-mail.

- ❑ When **sending e-mail**, do include a Subject line, and keep your messages brief.

- ❑ Documents can be sent by **e-mail** or **fax** directly from an Office 97 application if you have a modem or are on a local area network.

- ❑ You can **attach files** from any application to an e-mail message.

- ❑ **Hyperlinks** can be used to link to files stored in public folders, or to Web pages and files on the Internet.

Index